Lovers' Quarrels

Lovers' Quarrels

By Molière

*Translated into English verse
by Richard Wilbur*

Theatre Communications Group
New York
2009

Lovers' Quarrels is published by Theatre Communications Group, Inc., 520 Eighth Avenue, 24th Floor, New York, NY 10018–4156

This project is funded by the Sidney E. Frank Foundation.

This publication is made possible in part with public funds from the New York State Council on the Arts, a State Agency.

TCG books are exclusively distributed to the book trade by Consortium Book Sales and Distribution.

LIBRARY OF CONGRESS CATALOGING-IN-PUBLICATION DATA
Molière, 1622–1673.
[Dépit amoureux. English]
Lovers' quarrels / by Molière ; translated into English verse by Richard Wilbur.—
1st ed.
p. cm.
ISBN 978-1-55936-339-6
I. Wilbur, Richard, 1921–
II. Title.
PQ1830.D4E5   2009
842'.4—dc22   2009016306

Cover design by Chip Kidd
Cover image: Burstein Collection/Corbis
Text design and composition by Lisa Govan

First Edition, May 2009

Contents

Introduction

L overs' Quarrels (*Le Dépit amoureux*) was Molière's second verse comedy and had its premiere in 1656, at Béziers in Langue-doc, with the author playing the role of the irascible Albert. Two years later, when Molière's players returned to Paris and were installed in the Petit-Bourbon, they initially displeased the public by attempting a number of Corneille's tragedies, but salvaged that first season with two Molière farces. *The Bungler (L'Étourdi)* was successfully offered in November 1658, and *Lovers' Quarrels*, which followed in December, did quite as well. Together, the two plays brought in some money and created a following. Le Boulanger de Chalussay, in a dramatic satire against Molière (1670), was forced to concede that the latter play had drawn "ahs" from its audience:

> On all sides there were cheers, and everyone
> Cried, "That's how plays should be conceived and done!"

George Saintsbury wrote of *Lovers' Quarrels* that "nothing so good had yet been seen on the French stage, as the quarrels and reconciliations of the quartet of master, mistress, valet and soubrette." The scenes in question, involving Éraste, Lucile, Gros-René and Marinette, are in Molière's liveliest vein, and their tone and theme might put us in mind of Michael Drayton's famous sonnet "Since there's no help, come let us kiss and part," while for Molière's contemporaries they might have recalled a charming dialogic ode of Horace's (III, 9) in which two lovers reunite. The quarrel-and-reconciliation scenes have long been excerpted and combined, in France, to constitute a pleasing short version of the play. In the original text, however, they are ably interwoven with plot borrowings from such Italian sources as Nicolo Secchi's *L'Interesse,* to make a comedy of error, misunderstanding and intrigue.

Though the persons of the play are well provided with qualities (Éraste is jealous, Valère is rash, Mascarille is cowardly), it is plot, rather than character, in which the play's complexities lie. These are traceable, as we gradually discover, to something that happened some twenty years in the past. At that time a rich kinsman promised an inheritance to Albert and his family, provided that the child Albert's wife was carrying proved to be male; if that condition was not met, the money would go to Polidore, the father of Valère. When Albert's wife bore a girl child, Albert secretly and dishonestly exchanged it for the illegitimate male child of Ignès the flower girl. To his newly acquired son, Albert gave the name of Ascagne, and Ignès meanwhile placed her new daughter in the care of Frosine's mother, a wet nurse. Not long afterward, when Albert was out of town on business, the boy Ascagne died; the wife, fearing a violent reaction from Albert, then secretly retrieved her daughter from the wet nurse, transferred to her the name of Ascagne, and dressed her as a boy.

A score of years later, we find Ascagne still in male attire, and passing now for a young man; however, as she tells her confidante Frosine in Act Two, Scene 1, Cupid has penetrated her disguise and filled her woman's heart with love for Valère, who has vainly been courting her sister, Lucile. Pretending to be Lucile, Ascagne has had a succession of rendezvous with Valère, meeting him in a black veil and in the dark of night. On a fifth or sixth such occasion, she has deceived him into a secret marriage, in the darkling presence of a notary, a tailor and Valère's valet, Mascarille.

What now develops, in the play's present time, is an imbroglio or general mixup, deriving from past deceptions. The characters are entangled in a web of misapprehensions, and it is these that generate the atmosphere of the play and drive its action. Ascagne believes that her hoaxing marriage to Valère has made her his wife. Valère understandably believes that the same rite has wedded him secretly to Lucile. Éraste, who has won the favor of Lucile, is troubled by the complacent air of his defeated rival, and presses his jealous inquiries until Mascarille—honestly, but mistakenly—gives him seeming grounds for a breach which is not repaired until the fourth act. The falling-out and reconciliation of Éraste and Lucile is mirrored in the behavior of their servants, Gros-René and Marinette. Meanwhile, Valère mortally offends Lucile and her father by claiming to have married her, and might well incur a bloodier duel than the jesting one which awaits him in the final act. Nor are these all of the mistakings and confusions that animate the skits and comic turns of the play: Albert, quite incredibly, believes after twenty years of family life that his child Ascagne is male. That is made plain at the beginning of his scene with the tutor Métaphraste, which (like the later scene with Polidore) is a frenzy of mutual incomprehension.

Throughout *Lovers' Quarrels*, the caroming encounters of the characters lead to further complication, rather than understanding and resolution, and Frosine, who from the first has some of the answers, shares her knowledge with Ascagne alone. Her breakneck expository speech in Act Five, Scene 4 informs Ascagne that the work of disentanglement has been accomplished offstage by her and by Ignès, and such matters as Albert's long defrauding of Polidore are dismissed as settled. The play then proceeds to give us not leisurely explanations and rapprochements but yet another hoax, in which Valère must be fooled and then enlightened as to the sex of his dueling opponent.

It would be churlish to ask of a madcap play like *Lovers' Quarrels* that its every event seem probable, but more than one critic has questioned the suddenness with which Valère, on finding that Ascagne is a woman, is seized with wonder, love and pleasure. Sir John Vanbrugh's *The Mistake* (1706), a spirited prose adaptation of *Le Dépit amoureux* which re-situates the play in Spain, seeks to improve the final scene by a stage direction in which Camillo (i.e., Ascagne) *"kneels, and lets her periwig fall off."* This revelation of her sex and comeliness fills Lorenzo (i.e., Valère) with amazement; it also causes Lopez (Mascarille) to exclaim that she is indeed a "pretty one," and Isabel (Frosine) to make such mention of her "virtue, beauty, wit and love" that Lorenzo might seem to love her by acclamation. But perhaps it suffices that Molière's Valère has been portrayed throughout as impulsive, fiery and bold. In any case, I and whatever audiences may see this translation played will agree with Vanbrugh that Ascagne's feminine beauty must be revealed. I don't know whether, after Albert's, "Let her go and change," there may be time for her to change costume and return to the scene; but I am certain that, for the curtain call, she must be in woman's dress and irresistible.

—RW
Cummington, Massachusetts, 2005

Lovers' Quarrels

CHARACTERS

ÉRASTE (ay-RAHST), in love with Lucile
ALBERT (ahl-BEAR), father of Lucile and Ascagne
GROS-RENÉ (grow-reNAY), Éraste's valet
VALÈRE (vah-LARE), son of Polidore
LUCILE (loo-SEAL), daughter of Albert
MARINETTE (mah-ree-NET), Lucile's maid
POLIDORE (po-lee-DORE), father of Valère
FROSINE (fro-SEEN), confidante to Ascagne
MASCARILLE (mah-ska-REE), Valère's valet
MÉTAPHRASTE (may-ta-FRAST), a pedant
LA RAPIÈRE (lah-rah-PIERRE), a bravo
ASCAGNE (ah-SKAHN-ya), Albert's daughter, disguised as a man

SETTING

A city street.

Act One

Scene 1

Éraste, Gros-René.

ÉRASTE

Well, if you want to know, I feel oppressed
By nagging doubts which give my mind no rest.
I fear my amorous hopes have been betrayed,
Whatever you say. At times I'm even afraid
That my rival's purse has bought your loyalty,
Or that my love deceives both you and me.

GROS-RENÉ

With all respect, sir, for your troubled heart,
Your fear that I might play a traitor's part
Is wounding to my pride and honesty,
And shows no grasp of physiognomy.
Men of my round proportions, sir, are not

Regarded as the type to scheme and plot—
Which good opinion I shall not gainsay:
I'm a solid citizen in every way.
That I have been deceived could well be so;
It's possible; I don't believe it, though.
Try as I will, I cannot figure out
What grounds you have for being racked by doubt.
Lucile is clearly fond of you, I'd say,
And welcomes you at any hour of day,
Whereas Valère, the source of your anxiety,
Is now but rarely seen in her society.

ÉRASTE

Such logic doesn't comfort me; good Lord,
He who's most seen may not be most adored,
And a woman's sugared words may serve to cover
Her warmer feelings for another lover.
Valère, moreover, shows too little pain
To be a recently discarded swain;
Hearing the lady speaking fondly to me,
He's blithe, and cool, and anything but gloomy—
Which spoils my sense of triumph, mars my bliss,
Stirs up those doubts you urge me to dismiss,
Makes me mistrust my happiness, and feel
Unsure of the sincerity of Lucile.
How it would simplify my life if he,
My rival, were consumed with jealousy!
If he would show a normal gloom and grief,
T'would ease my mind and give my thoughts relief.
Don't you, too, think it strange that he can be
So blithe about a rival's victory?
Do you not see, then, why I brood upon
The matter, and try to guess what's going on?

4

GROS-RENÉ

Perhaps he found a new love when the old
Rejected him, and so feels quite consoled.

ÉRASTE

A man who's been rejected would not pay
Blithe visits to the lady every day.
No, after a rebuff so grave and sore,
He could not wait upon her anymore.
One can't be cool when in the presence of
The heartless person whom one used to love:
Either one feels a sullen anger, or
One's jilted passion flares up as before.
However well an old flame's been suppressed,
There's still some jealousy in the lover's breast,
So that he can't look on without chagrin
While a rival claims the prize he couldn't win.

GROS-RENÉ

Such theorizing, sir, is not for me:
I put my trust in what my eyes can see,
And I'm not so fond of misery that I
Will fret and mope without good reasons why.
Why deal in dire conjectures, and rehearse
Dark arguments that make my mood the worse?
Why yield to baseless doubt and mere suspicion?
Don't look for trouble, say I. That's my position.
Grief, in my judgment, is a sorry state;
Without good cause, I want none on my plate,
And even when good causes can be had,
It goes against my nature to be sad.
In love, sir, our two destinies intertwine:
Your amorous fortune will determine mine,
For if the lady broke her faith to you,

Her lady's maid would send me packing, too.
I do my best, though, not to think about it.
If she says, "I love you," I refuse to doubt it,
Nor shall I judge the happiness of my lot
By whether Mascarille is glum or not.
So long as Marinette will be so kind
As to kiss and hug me when I'm so inclined,
My rival's free to laugh his head off, while
I match him laugh for laugh in the same style,
And we shall see whose laugh sounds more sincere.

ÉRASTE

Well, that's your nature.

GROS-RENÉ

But look, she's drawing near.

Scene 2

Éraste, Marinette, Gros-René.

GROS-RENÉ

Psst! Marinette!

MARINETTE

Ooh! What are you doing there?

GROS-RENÉ

We were discussing you, my lady fair.

MARINETTE

(To Éraste:)
So you're here, too, sir! You've made me run about
Like a headless chicken, and I'm tuckered out.

ÉRASTE

Oh? Why?

MARINETTE

I've covered miles and miles of ground,
And I guarantee you . . .

ÉRASTE

What?

MARINETTE

That you can't be found
At home, or church, or plaza, or café.

GROS-RENÉ

Well, that's a safe conclusion.

ÉRASTE

But tell me, pray,
Who sent you looking for me?

MARINETTE

Someone who
Is far from being ill-disposed toward you;
In short, my mistress.

ÉRASTE

Marinette, my dear,
If you're her heart's true oracle and seer,
Keep no dark secrets from me, I implore you.
Tell me—it won't affect my feelings for you—
Could your lovely mistress so deceive my zeal
As to pretend a love she doesn't feel?

MARINETTE

Lord! How can you dream up such silly stuff?
Hasn't she made her sentiments clear enough?
What more assurance could your heart require?
What do you want?

GROS-RENÉ

He'd have his heart's desire
If Valère would hang himself from the nearest tree.

MARINETTE

Why so?

GROS-RENÉ

He's jealous to the nth degree.

MARINETTE

What, of Valère? That notion is insane,
And must have issued from a feverish brain.
(To Éraste:)
I've always thought you sensible, and till now
I've sensed an intellect behind that brow,
But it appears that I was much misled.
(To Gros-René:)
Do you, too, have a fever in your head?

GROS-RENÉ

Me, jealous? God forbid that such a state
Of foolish grief should cause me to lose weight!
I trust in your fidelity, and my
Opinion of myself, love, is so high,
I'm sure I have no equal on this earth.
Where could you find a man of greater worth?

8

MARINETTE

Well said: A lover ought to talk that way—
None of these doubts that jealous men display!
All that one gains by them's a loss of face
That lets your rival pass you in the race.
Envy will often open a mistress' eyes
To the merits of the man with whom one vies,
And I know one such man, whose happy fate
Owes everything to a rival's jealous hate.
In matters of the heart, no man of sense
Ever displays a lack of confidence.
Don't make yourself unhappy, sir, for naught.
Those are some truths I felt you should be taught.

ÉRASTE

Enough, now. Tell me what you've come to tell.

MARINETTE

Sir, you deserve to suffer for a spell,
And I should punish you by some delay
In giving you the news I've brought today.
But come, take this, and banish doubt and fear.
Read it aloud: There's none but us to hear.

ÉRASTE

(Reading:)
"You told me that there was no task
Your love would not perform at my command.
Pray, prove your love this very day, and ask
My father for his daughter's hand.
Tell him my heart is ready to
Be yours, as I now give you leave to say.
If then he orders me to marry you,

I promise you that I'll obey."
Oh, joy! You are a heavenly messenger,
For bringing me these loving words from her.

GROS-RENÉ

I told you all was well, but you wouldn't be shaken.
It isn't often, sir, that I'm mistaken.

ÉRASTE

(Reading again:)
"Tell him my heart is ready to
Be yours, as I now give you leave to say.
If he orders me to marry you,
I promise you that I'll obey."

MARINETTE

If I told her of your dark suspicions, she
Would disavow those words, believe you me.

ÉRASTE

Oh, pray don't tell her of my passing mood
Of foolish worry and incertitude:
Or if you tell her, kindly add that I'm
Prepared to die to expiate that crime—
That if I have offended her, I desire
To sacrifice my life to her just ire.

MARINETTE

Well, let's not talk of dying; it's early yet.

ÉRASTE

In any case, I'm greatly in your debt,
And I assure you that I'll soon repay
My pretty messenger in some handsome way.

MARINETTE

Ah, that reminds me. There was another scene
Where I looked for you just now.

ÉRASTE

Eh?

MARINETTE

The place I mean
Is near the market.

ÉRASTE

Oh?

MARINETTE

The shop, you know,
Where you so kindly promised, a month ago,
To buy a ring for me.

ÉRASTE

Ah, yes! Quite true.

GROS-RENÉ

Sly wench!

ÉRASTE

I've been too slow in giving you
The little gift I promised to confer.
But . . .

MARINETTE

Heavens! I didn't mean to press you, sir.

GROS-RENÉ

Oh, *no!*

ÉRASTE

(*Giving her his own ring:*)
　　If this ring pleases you, why not
Take it in place of the one that I forgot?

MARINETTE

Oh, sir, I'd be ashamed to take your ring.

GROS-RENÉ

Go on and take it, you poor shamefaced thing.
Only a fool declines a gift, say I.

MARINETTE

I'll wear it to recall your kindness by.

ÉRASTE

When may I see my angel, my future bride?

MARINETTE

First, you must get her father on your side.

ÉRASTE

But what if he rejects me?

MARINETTE

　　Then we'll do
Whatever it takes to gain her hand for you.
She must be yours, and to achieve that aim
You'll do your utmost, and we'll do the same.

ÉRASTE

Farewell: By sundown, then, we'll know our fate.

12

(Éraste rereads the letter, sotto voce.)

MARINETTE

(To Gros-René:)
Well, what about *our* love? What say you, mate?
You haven't yet proposed.

GROS-RENÉ

    For folks like us,
Marriage can be arranged without a fuss.
I want you; will you marry me?

MARINETTE

    With pleasure.

GROS-RENÉ

Let's shake.

MARINETTE

    Farewell then, Gros-René, my treasure.

GROS-RENÉ

Farewell, my star.

MARINETTE

    Farewell, my cupid's dart.

GROS-RENÉ

Farewell, sweet comet, rainbow of my heart.
(Exit Marinette.)
Thank Heaven! We both have reason for good cheer.
Albert will not refuse you, never fear.

ÉRASTE

Here comes Valère, now.

GROS-RENÉ

Knowing what we know,
I pity the poor wretch.

Scene 3

Valère, Éraste, Gros-René.

ÉRASTE

Well, Valère! Hello!

VALÈRE

Well, well, Éraste!

ÉRASTE

How goes your love life, eh?

VALÈRE

How's your tender passion?

ÉRASTE

Stronger every day.

VALÈRE

Mine too grows stronger.

ÉRASTE

For Lucile?

VALÈRE

Why, yes.

ÉRASTE

Well you're a paragon of doggedness,
I'm forced to say.

VALÈRE

Your stubborn constancy
Should be a model to posterity.

ÉRASTE

I'm not, myself, the sort of lover who
Will settle for a friendly smile or two,
And my devotion isn't strong enough
To overlook rejection and rebuff:
In short, I like to see my love requited.

VALÈRE

Why, so do I. In that we stand united.
However fair she is, I cannot burn
For one who doesn't love me in return.

ÉRASTE

And yet Lucile—

VALÈRE

Lucile, whom I adore,
Has given me all my heart could wish, and more.

ÉRASTE

You don't ask much, in other words.

VALÈRE

Oh, yes,
Far more than you suppose.

ÉRASTE

I, nonetheless,
Have grounds for feeling that I've won her heart.

VALÈRE

In which, dear fellow, I play the leading part.

ÉRASTE

Come, don't deceive yourself.

VALÈRE

Come, come. You'll find
That credulous desire has made you blind.

ÉRASTE

If I dared show you proof of her complete
Devotion . . . But no, your heart would cease to beat.

VALÈRE

If I dared disclose a certain fact . . . But no,
I mustn't tell; you couldn't bear the blow.

ÉRASTE

Really, you go too far in mocking me.
I'm forced to puncture your complacency.
Read this,

VALÈRE

(Having read the letter:)
How sweet.

ÉRASTE

You recognize the hand?

VALÈRE

Yes, it's Lucile's.

ÉRASTE

Well! Now you understand—

VALÈRE

(Laughing as he leaves.)
Farewell, Éraste.

GROS-RENÉ

He's mad, beyond a doubt.
What can the fellow see to laugh about?

ÉRASTE

I'm stunned by his behavior; baffled by it.
Some devilish mystery must underlie it.

GROS-RENÉ

Here comes his servant.

ÉRASTE

Let's trick him, and discover
Some clue to his master's conduct as a lover.

Scene 4

Éraste, Mascarille, Gros-René.

MASCARILLE

(Aside:)
Yes, to serve a young man who is daft with love
Is a thankless job that one gets weary of.

17

GROS-RENÉ

Hello.

MASCARILLE

Hello.

GROS-RENÉ

What's Mascarille doing today?
Is he coming back? Is he going? Or will he stay?

MASCARILLE

I can't come back, for I've not yet been there. Nor
Am I going, for I've stopped to talk. What's more,
I cannot stay, because this instant I
Must take my leave of you.

ÉRASTE

A neat reply.
Wait, Mascarille.

MASCARILLE

Ah. Yes, sir. At your service.

ÉRASTE

My, how you scampered off! Do I make you nervous?

MASCARILLE

I need not fear a gentleman so kind.

ÉRASTE

Shake, then. Let's put old jealousies out of mind.
We're friends, now. I concede the lady to
Your master, and wish all joy to him and you.

MASCARILLE

You mean it?

ÉRASTE

I've a brand-new passion. Ask Gros-René.

GROS-RENÉ

That's so. Marinette is yours now, needless to say.

MASCARILLE

Never mind that. Our little rivalry
Is not the battle of the century.
But you, sir, have you truly ceased to court
The lady, or did you merely speak in sport?

ÉRASTE

When I saw success would crown your master's suit,
I felt it would be foolish to dispute
The prize of her affections anymore.

MASCARILLE

I'm much relieved by what you say. Though for
A time we rather feared that you might win,
It's very wise that you should now give in.
Yes, you do well to leave a lady whose
Fond treatment of yourself was but a ruse:
A thousand times, sir, knowing what I knew,
I grieved to see false hopes aroused in you.
So to deceive a good man is a shame.
But how on earth did you see through their game?
When they exchanged their vows, no one was by
Save darkest night, two witnesses, and I,
And, until now, their nuptials seemed to be
Enshrouded in a perfect secrecy.

ÉRASTE

What are you saying?

MASCARILLE

That I am much surprised,
And cannot guess by whom you were advised
That, under false pretenses which misled
Both you and everyone, they chose to wed
In secret, so intense their passions were.

ÉRASTE

You lie!

MASCARILLE

Quite so. Whatever you prefer.

ÉRASTE

You're a scoundrel.

MASCARILLE

So I am.

ÉRASTE

What you deserve
Is a hundred lashes for this bit of nerve.

MASCARILLE

Do what you will.

ÉRASTE

Ah, Gros-René

GROS-RENÉ

I'm here.

ÉRASTE

The lie he told me may be true, I fear.
(To Mascarille:)
Don't try to run.

MASCARILLE

No.

ÉRASTE

Lucile is married, you say—

MASCARILLE

No, I was joking, sir.

ÉRASTE

You were joking, eh?

MASCARILLE

No, I wasn't joking.

ÉRASTE

Then it's true?

MASCARILLE

No, no!
I don't say that.

ÉRASTE

What *do* you say?

MASCARILLE

Oh, woe!
I shall say nothing, and play it safe.

ÉRASTE

Decide
Whether it's true, or whether you have lied.

MASCARILLE

Sir, have it any way you like. I dare
Not differ with you.

ÉRASTE

(*Drawing his sword:*)
Tell me, or I swear
That I shall loosen up your tongue with this.

MASCARILLE

If I spoke again, I'd only speak amiss.
I beg you, sir, to take a stick and give
Me twenty thumps as an alternative,
And let me then get out of here intact.

ÉRASTE

Tell me the truth, the plain and simple fact,
Or you shall die.

MASCARILLE

Oh, dear! I shall obey you,
But don't be angry with me, sir, I pray you.

ÉRASTE

Speak. But be very careful what you do,
If you utter just one word that isn't true.
Nothing shall save you from my righteous fury.

MASCARILLE

You may break my bones, sir, or as judge and jury,
Condemn me to be stabbed until I'm dead,
If there's the least untruth in what I've said.

ÉRASTE

Then they're really married?

MASCARILLE

   I spoke unguardedly
In that connection, as I've come to see:
But yes, the fact is, sir, that you are right.
After five days in which they met each night
And you were used as cover for their plot,
Day before yesterday they tied the knot.
Lucile has taken care to hide thereafter
Her powerful affection for my master,
Knowing that he would sensibly construe
The warmth and favor she might show to you
As a bit of prudent camouflage, whereby
To keep their secret from the general eye.
If you don't believe me, sir, let Gros-René
Accompany me some night. I'll lead the way
And show him how my master, in the shady
Hours, has free access to the lady.

ÉRASTE

Get out of my sight, you swine!

MASCARILLE

(Going.)
   Sir, I'm not loath
To take my leave.

ÉRASTE

Well, well.

GROS-RENÉ

Well, sir, we've both
Been taken in, if he can be believed.

ÉRASTE

Alas, it's all too true. I've been deceived.
His tale makes sense of everything, God knows.
Valère's reaction to this letter shows
How he and that false girl are hand in glove.
This letter's just some trick to hide their love.

Scene 5

Éraste, Marinette, Gros-René.

MARINETTE

My mistress tells me that toward evening, sir,
She will be in her garden. Pray call on her.

ÉRASTE

You two-faced creature! How dare you speak to me?
Go, go; and let your mistress know that she
Need bother me no more with billets-doux.
Here's what I think of them, and her, and you.

(He tears up the letter and exits.)

MARINETTE

Well, Gros-René! What's eating him? Tell me what—

GROS-RENÉ

How dare you speak to me, you wicked slut?
You crocodile, whose treachery has outdone
The savage, man-devouring Laestrygon!
Go, go to your mistress now, and say that we,
Despite her cunning and duplicity,
Are duped by her no longer, and that the pair
Of you may go to Hell, for all we care.

MARINETTE

(Alone:)
Poor Marinette! If I've not been dreaming, then
What awful demon has possessed these men?
When I tell my mistress, how it will upset her!
What a rude answer to a loving letter!

Act Two

Scene 1

Ascagne, Frosine.

FROSINE

Ascagne, confide in me. I'll be discreet.

ASCAGNE

Is it safe to broach such matters in the street?
We must take care lest curious folk come near us,
Or someone at a window overhear us.

FROSINE

Even at home, we're not so safe as this:
There's nothing round us that our eyes could miss.
Here, we may talk in perfect privacy.

ASCAGNE

Ah, where to begin? This is so hard for me.

FROSINE

Your secret is a weighty one, I judge.

ASCAGNE

Indeed it is; it's one that I begrudge
Even to you, and would not tell you now
Unless I had to.

FROSINE

How you wrong me! How
Can you hesitate to open up your heart
To one who's kept your secrets from the start,
To one who grew up at your side, and who
Was ever reticent concerning you,
Who knows why . . .

ASCAGNE

Yes, you know the strange, complex
Reasons why I must hide my birth and sex.
You know that in our household I was bred
To replace the boy Ascagne, who was dead,
And by that ruse retain a legacy
Which others would inherit, but for me.
Because you know these things, I'm free to share
My thoughts with you, and lay my feelings bare.
But first, Frosine, do let me have your view
Of a question which I find no answer to.
Was Albert no party to the fairy tale
That he's my father, and that my sex is male?

FROSINE

To tell the truth, this question that you raise
Is one I've never fathomed; it's like a maze
That leads me nowhere; I'm bewildered by it,
Nor could my mother help me clarify it.
Here's all I know: The dear son of Albert,
Even before his birth, had been made heir
To a large fortune, left him by a late
Uncle whose wealth and properties were great.
When that son died, his mother kept it back
From her absent husband, fearing a heart attack
If he saw the hoped-for legacy miscarry
And pass to another beneficiary.
To hide her child's death, she decided to
Replace him with another, and soon found you
At my family's house, where you'd been put to nurse.
Your mother, doubtless for a generous purse,
Agreed to the hoax, and promised not to tell,
And others, I believe, were bribed as well.
We never told Albert. His wife confined
The truth for twelve years in her secret mind,
Then died so suddenly that there was not
A chance for her to tell him of the plot.
However, he has kept in touch, I gather,
With a woman whom I know to be your mother,
And evidently helps her on the sly.
If he does so, there must be a reason why.
On the other hand, he wishes you to marry
A girl he's chosen, and that's extraordinary.
Do you think he knows that you replaced his son,
Yet doesn't know your gender? Well, let's be done
With this digression; I've rambled on, I fear.
Tell me your secret, which I long to hear.

ASCAGNE

Cupid, my dear, can't be deceived. His eyes
Have penetrated this, my male disguise,
And through these garments sent his subtle dart
Into a maiden's vulnerable heart,
I am in love.

FROSINE

In love!

ASCAGNE

Frosine, don't let
Yourself give in to wonderment just yet;
Be still, and let my trembling heart advise you
Of something that will even more surprise you.

FROSINE

What is it?

ASCAGNE

I love Valère.

FROSINE

Good Lord! You love
A man whose family has been cheated of
A fortune by your male disguise, and who,
If he divined the truth regarding you,
Would claim that legacy without delay!
This is indeed astounding, I must say.

ASCAGNE

But I've something still more wondrous to confess:
I am his wife.

FROSINE

His wife? Do you mean it?

ASCAGNE

Yes.

FROSINE

Oh! That's a shock I wasn't ready for.
My head is reeling.

ASCAGNE

Wait; there's something more.

FROSINE

There's more?

ASCAGNE

I am indeed his wife, but he
Knows nothing of my true identity.

FROSINE

Well, I give up. I'm overcome. You win.
All these surprises cause my head to spin,
And such a riddle's too much for my brain.

ASCAGNE

Then listen patiently, and I'll explain.
When Valère came suing for my sister's hand,
He seemed to be a worthy suitor, and,
Seeing his passionate appeals denied,
My sympathies were all upon his side.
I wished Lucile would fall beneath his spell;
I thought her cold, and pled his cause so well
That helplessly my heart began to stir
With the feelings he could not arouse in her.

When he spoke to her, 'twas my heart that was captured;
When he sighed in vain, 'twas I who was enraptured,
And those professions she could not return
Conquered my soul and made my spirit yearn.
You see, Frosine, how my frail heart was hit
By amorous darts which were not meant for it,
How love's deflected arrows pierced my breast
And I returned that love with interest.
After a time, my dear, the moment came
When I spoke my love, though in another's name.
Pretending, one dark night, to be Lucile,
I told Valère what I had come to feel,
And feigned so well that he did not see through
The part I played in that dark interview,
Thus, speaking as Lucile, I pleased his ear
By whispering in it that I held him dear,
But that my father favored an alliance
With someone else, and I must feign compliance;
That we must therefore hide our love from sight,
Letting our only witness be the night,
And that, lest we should give ourselves away,
We must avoid all private talk by day;
That, as before this meeting, I would be
Cool and indifferent in his company,
And that, on both our parts, no act or word
Should lead the world to guess what had occurred.
Well, not to dwell on every calculation
Which forwarded my bold impersonation,
It worked so well at last that I acquired,
As I have said, the husband I desired.

FROSINE

My, my! What hidden talents you possess!
From your cool exterior, one would never guess.

32

But isn't it rather rash, the thing you've done?
Although your plot's successfully begun,
How can it possibly end? Have you thought about
What soon must happen, when the truth comes out?

ASCAGNE

When love is strong enough, the lover's soul
Will stop at nothing to attain its goal,
And, once it has achieved that happy end,
It doesn't care what else the Fates may send.
There now, I've told you everything, my dear.
Advise me. Ah, but look! My husband's here.

Scene 2

Valère, Ascagne, Frosine.

VALÈRE

My friends, if by my presence I would balk
Your wish to have a confidential talk,
I shan't disturb you.

ASCAGNE

Oh, by all means do,
For what we were discussing, sir, was you.

VALÈRE

Me?

ASCAGNE

You.

33

VALÈRE

Well!

ASCAGNE

I was saying that Valère,
Were I a woman, could teach my heart to care,
And that if he were fond of me, he'd find
How very quickly I'd respond in kind.

VALÈRE

Such flattering things are easy enough to say
When such an obstacle is in the way;
But if you had a magic change of gender,
I doubt your feelings would be quite so tender.

ASCAGNE

Oh yes, they would! And if you'd have me, then
I'd make you, sir, the happiest of men.

VALÈRE

If you want to make me happy, will you aid me
By interceding with a certain lady?

ASCAGNE

I fear I couldn't make myself do that.

VALÈRE

Hmm. Your refusal's rather brusque and flat.

ASCAGNE

Come! What did you expect of me, Valère?
Were I a woman, and loved you, would it be fair
To make me promise that I'd do my part

To help you win another woman's heart?
No, that's a painful task I could not do.

 VALÈRE

But since you're not a woman . . .

ASCAGNE

What I said to you
Was spoken as a woman, and must be
So understood.

VALÈRE

Well then, Ascagne, I see
That I can't appeal to your goodwill unless
Heaven alters you, and bids you wear a dress.
Unless you're a woman, your feelings for me fade,
And you see no cause to offer me your aid.

ASCAGNE

I'm most particular, and it doesn't suit me
When those who love don't do so absolutely,
With all their hearts. I tell you quite sincerely
That I shan't help you unless you very clearly
State, in a manner simple, frank and true,
That you're as fond of me as I of you,
That you return my friendship very strongly,
And that, were I a woman, you'd never wrong me
By wishing for another woman's hand.

VALÈRE

I've never heard so jealous a demand!
But since I value your affection, I
Shall swear to all the things you specify.

ASCAGNE

Sincerely?

VALÈRE

Yes, sincerely.

ASCAGNE

In that case, I'm
Prepared to serve you, friend, at any time.

VALÈRE

I've a great secret which I'll soon confide
To you, and I shall need you on my side.

ASCAGNE

And I've a secret, too, which when confessed
Will put your feelings for me to the test.

VALÈRE

Hmm. What's this mystery that you must conceal?

ASCAGNE

That I'm in love—with whom, I can't reveal;
And that, through your great influence with this
Belovèd of mine, you might secure my bliss.

VALÈRE

Who is it, Ascagne? I'll do what I must do
To bring you happiness, I promise you.

ASCAGNE

Ah, what a fatal promise you have made!

VALÈRE

Come, tell me what belovèd I must persuade.

ASCAGNE

No, it's too soon to tell. The person, though,
Is close to you.

VALÈRE

How wonderful; if so,
I pray that it's my sister . . .

ASCAGNE

I can't yet say.

VALÈRE

Why not?

ASCAGNE

I have my reasons for delay.
When you tell your secret, I'll tell mine to you.

VALÈRE

I can't, unless another permits me to.

ASCAGNE

Then get permission, and once each secret's heard,
We'll see which one can better keep his word.

VALÈRE

Farewell, then. We are agreed.

ASCAGNE

Agreed, Valère.

FROSINE

He wants your brotherly help, I do declare.

Scene 3

Lucile, Ascagne, Frosine, Marinette.

LUCILE
(Speaking the first three lines to Marinette:)
Yes, yes, that's how I shall retaliate;
The joy of giving pain to one I hate
Is all I hope to gain by this decision.
Brother, my plans have undergone revision.
Valère, though I long took no notice of him,
Attracts me now, and I propose to love him.

ASCAGNE
Good heavens, Sister! Why this sudden change?
Your inconsistency is very strange.

LUCILE
And yours, I must say, puzzles me still more.
You were Valère's great advocate before;
You strongly pled his cause, accusing me
Of pride, caprice, injustice, cruelty:
But now, when I would love him, you protest,
And speak to me against his interest!

ASCAGNE
It's in *your* interest that I speak. I know
That someone else now has his heart in tow.
I fear that your proud feelings would be bruised
If you sought to lure him back, and he refused.

LUCILE
If that's your only worry, never fear.
To me, his heart's desires are very clear,

And his fond looks can easily be read;
Yes, you may safely tell him what I've said;
Or if you won't, I'll tell him on my own
That I'm touched by the devotion he has shown.
Speak, Brother. Can my decision so dismay you?

ASCAGNE

Oh, Sister, if I've any power to sway you,
If you will harken to a brother's prayer,
Forget this notion, and do not steal Valère
From a young girl whose cause is dear to me,
And who, in truth, deserves your sympathy.
The poor thing loves him madly, and has made known
The secrets of her heart to me alone,
With such warm feeling as might melt the pride
Of any rival, and make her step aside.
Yes, you'd take pity on her if you knew
What grief this whim of yours could drive her to;
And I, who know her heart, can testify,
Dear Sister, that the girl will surely die
If the man whom she adores is stolen by you.
Éraste's the swain who ought to satisfy you;
Your mutual fondness . . .

LUCILE

Brother, say no more.
I don't know who it is you're pleading for,
But do, please, let this declamation cease,
And leave me to collect my thoughts in peace.

ASCAGNE

Ah, cruel Sister! If, in this affair,
You do as you have threatened, I shall despair.

Scene 4

Lucile, Marinette.

MARINETTE

Well! Your decision, madam, was quick indeed.

LUCILE

A heart that has been wronged reacts with speed:
It hastens to get even, and assuage
By any means its bitterness and rage.
The monster! How could he insult me so?

MARINETTE

That question baffles me; I just don't know.
I brood and brood upon the mystery,
But his strange behavior still is Greek to me.
I've never seen a man so overjoyed
By happy news; his bliss was unalloyed;
He read your note with purest happiness
And called me a "heavenly messenger," no less.
But when I brought your second message, who'd
Have dreamt that he could be so harsh and rude?
I cannot guess what happened in between
Those messages to make him turn so mean.

LUCILE

Whatever happened can't extenuate
His actions, or defend him from my hate.
Why seek some explanation other than
The viciousness and baseness of the man?
After that gracious letter which I sent,
What could excuse a wrath so violent?

MARINETTE

You're right, of course. His unprovoked attack
Was simple treason; he's stabbed you in the back.
Madam, we've both been had: Shall we allow
These scurvy rascals to deceive us now
With pretty words, and take advantage of us?
Shall we allow these dogs to say they love us,
And in our weakness yield to them again?
No, no! Enough of folly! Enough of men!

LUCILE

Well, let him boast of how he's done me wrong;
I shall not let him smirk and gloat for long.
He'll see how shallow fickleness is borne
By a noble heart, and brushed aside with scorn.

MARINETTE

In our position, one can at least be glad
Not to be in the power of some cad.
I used my head, one night, when I declined
To do the things that someone had in mind.
Another girl, in hopes of marriage, might
Have yielded to temptation on that night,
But I said *nescio vos.*

LUCILE

      Be serious, please.
This is no time for trivialities.
Listen to me: My heart is racked with pain,
And should it happen that this faithless swain,
Through a happy turn of fortune which I would
Be foolish, now, to think a likelihood
(Since Heaven too much enjoys my persecution
To let me have the joy of retribution):

If ever, I say, the Fates should lead him to
Grovel before me, as he ought to do,
And groan that he does not deserve to live,
Don't plead for him and urge me to forgive.
No, no, I'd have you zealously remind me
That he has used me basely and unkindly,
And even if I'm tempted to relent
And let that scoundrel play the penitent,
Bid me preserve my hatred and my pride,
And not allow my anger to subside.

MARINETTE

Count on me, madam; I fully share your view,
I am at least as furious as you,
And I had rather die a virgin than
Be reconciled with that fat, treacherous man.
If he dared . . .

Scene 5

Albert, Lucile, Marinette.

ALBERT

Lucile, go tell the tutor, dear,
That I wish to have a word with him out here.
Since he's Ascagne's master, perhaps he'll know
Why my son's spirits seem to be so low.
(Alone:)
One guilty deed, and life becomes a sea
Of dread, and worry, and anxiety!
Since I brought up a stranger's child, pretending
That he was mine, my cares have been unending.

Greed made me do it, and it's brought such woe,
I wish I'd never thought of doing so.
Sometimes I fear the fraud will be detected,
Leaving my household poor and unrespected.
Sometimes my son, whom I must shield from harm,
Seems ringed with dangers, and I feel alarm.
If I leave town on business for a day,
I fear that folk, when I return, will say,
"Alas! You haven't heard? Your son's in bed
With a chill, or a broken leg, or a bandaged head."
In short, I lead a life of strain and tension,
Where every moment's full of apprehension.
Ah!

Scene 6

Albert, Métaphraste.

MÉTAPHRASTE

Mandatum tuum curo diligenter.

ALBERT

Master . . .

MÉTAPHRASTE

The root of "Master" is *magister,*
Which means "three times as great."

ALBERT

That's news to me,
I'm bound to say. However, let it be.
Now, Master . . .

MÉTAPHRASTE

Proceed.

ALBERT

I mean to, never fear.
But don't proceed to interrupt me, hear?
Now, once more, Master (this is my third try),
I'm worried about my son; you know how I
Have cherished him, and brought him up to be . . .

MÉTAPHRASTE

Quite so: *Fílio non potest praeferri*
Nisi fílius.

ALBERT

When we talk, Master, I wish
That you'd spare me all that pointless gibberish.
You're a fine Latin scholar, your learning's great,
Or so I have been told, at any rate,
But in our conversation here today
Don't put your erudition on display
And shower me with verbiage, as if you
Were in some pulpit, and I were in a pew.
My father was a clever man of affairs,
But he taught me nothing save my Latin prayers,
Which I have said for fifty years without
The least idea of what they're all about.
So set aside your fancy lore, and please
Adjust your speech to my deficiencies.

MÉTAPHRASTE

So be it.

ALBERT

My son displays no interest

In marriage; whatever match I may suggest,
He's strangely cold, and disinclined to wed.

MÉTAPHRASTE

Perhaps what Marcus Tullius' brother said
To Atticus applies, sir, to your son;
The Greeks, moreover, say *Athanaton* . . .

ALBERT

Incorrigible pedant! Will you please
Forget these Greeks, Albanians, Portuguese,
And all your other tribes and populations.
What has my son to do with foreign nations?

MÉTAPHRASTE

Very well, then. Your son . . .

ALBERT

                    His looks suggest
That a secret flame may burn within his breast:
There's something on his mind, it's safe to say;
Unmarked by him, I saw him yesterday
In a part of the woods where folk are seldom seen.

MÉTAPHRASTE

"A remote place in the woods," is what you mean,
"A secluded spot." The Latin is *secessus*.
As Virgil put it, *est in secessu locus*.

ALBERT

How could this Virgil say a thing like that?
Those woods were lonely, and I'll eat my hat
If anyone was there except us two.

MÉTAPHRASTE

I mentioned Virgil as a poet who
Employed a phrase beside which yours was crude,
Not as a witness of the scene you viewed.

ALBERT

And what I say to you is: What in blazes
Do I want with poets, witnesses and phrases?
One witness is enough. Don't be absurd.

MÉTAPHRASTE

Yet it is wise to use the terms preferred
By the best authors. *Tu vivendo bonos,*
As the saying goes, *scribendo sequare peritos.*

ALBERT

The fiend won't listen! He's stubborn as an ox.

MÉTAPHRASTE

That was Quintilian's teaching, sir.

ALBERT

                    A pox
Upon this chatterer!

MÉTAPHRASTE

            He also wrote,
On the same theme, a jest which I shall quote
For your delight.

ALBERT

        It would delight me, knave,
To hurl you down to Hades. How I crave
To put a gag upon that ugly snout!

MÉTAPHRASTE

What is it that you're so upset about?
What do you want?

ALBERT

I want to be listened to,
As I've told you twenty times.

MÉTAPHRASTE

Of course you do,
And if that's all, your wish is my command:
I'm silent.

ALBERT

You had better be.

MÉTAPHRASTE

Here I stand,
Ready to listen.

ALBERT

Good.

MÉTAPHRASTE

May I expire
If I say one word!

ALBERT

God grant you that desire!

MÉTAPHRASTE

You'll be no longer troubled by my prating.

ALBERT

So be it!

MÉTAPHRASTE
Speak when you wish, sir.

ALBERT
I've been waiting . . .

MÉTAPHRASTE
And I won't interrupt you, never fear,

ALBERT
Enough.

MÉTAPHRASTE
My promise to you was sincere.

ALBERT
No doubt.

MÉTAPHRASTE
I told you that I would be still.

ALBERT
Yes.

MÉTAPHRASTE
Henceforth I'll be mute.

ALBERT
I'm sure you will.

MÉTAPHRASTE
Take heart, now; speak; I'm all attention, sir.
You can't say now that I'm a jabberer:
I'll make no sound, not even a cough or sneeze.

ALBERT

(Aside:)
The villain!

MÉTAPHRASTE

But don't be too long-winded, please.
I've listened all this time, and it's only right
That I should speak a while.

ALBERT

Damned blatherskite!

MÉTAPHRASTE

What! Must I listen to you forever? No,
Let's share the talking, sir, or I shall go.

ALBERT

My patience is . . .

MÉTAPHRASTE

Good God! Still talking, is he?
When will it end? His chatter makes me dizzy!

ALBERT

I haven't said . . .

MÉTAPHRASTE

Ah! Has he no remorse?
Nothing can stem the flood of his discourse!

ALBERT

This is too much!

MÉTAPHRASTE

What torture! Please, no more.
Come, let me speak a little, I implore.
Unless he speaks, a wise man might as well
Be foolish.

ALBERT

I'm going to silence him, by Hell.

(Exit.)

MÉTAPHRASTE

A great philosopher said long ago,
"Speak, that you may be known." That's apropos,
And I would think it better to have ceased
To be a man, and changed into a beast,
Than to be cheated of my right to speak.
Oh, I shall have a headache for a week . . .
How I detest these babbling fools! My word!
Yes, if the sage and learnèd are not heard,
If the wise man can't impart what he has learned,
The order of the world is overturned:
The fox shall be devoured by the hen;
Children shall be the teachers of old men;
The lamb shall crush the wolf between its jaws;
Women shall fight, and madmen make the laws;
Denounced by crooks, the judges shall be tried,
And boys at school shall tan the master's hide;
The sick shall give the well their medicine;
The timid hare . . .
(Albert reenters, clangs a large cowbell in Métaphraste's ear, and drives him off.)
No! No! Help; what a din!

Act Three

Scene 1

Mascarille.

MASCARILLE

Fate sometimes favors boldness, and a man
Must save his neck in any way he can.
Once I had slipped, and given away the show,
The one trick I could think of was to go
Posthaste to our old master Polidore
And fill him in on what had gone before.
His son's a violent man whose rage I dread,
And if his rival told him what I've said,
Good God! How I'd be knocked about, and mauled!
However, such a scene could be forestalled
If these old gentlemen would talk, and see
Their way to calm the waters and agree.

That's why I'm here. I've come to ask Albert
To meet with Polidore on this affair.

(He knocks on Albert's door.)

Scene 2

Albert, Mascarílle.

ALBERT

Who knocks?

MASCARILLE

A friend.

ALBERT

What brings you here today,
Mascarille?

MASCARILLE

I've come here, sir, to say
Good morning . . .

ALBERT

You're good to take the trouble. I
Too say good morning.

(Goes back inside.)

MASCARILLE

Well, there's a brusque reply.
What a rude man!

52

(Knocks.)

ALBERT

Still here?

MASCARILLE

I wasn't through.

ALBERT

Didn't you say good morning?

MASCARILLE

Yes, that's true.

ALBERT

Well then, good morning.

(He turns to go; Mascarille detains him.)

MASCARILLE

Yes, but I also came
From Polidore, to greet you in his name.

ALBERT

Ah! Your master sent you, then? You were assigned
To bring me his good wishes?

MASCARILLE

Yes.

ALBERT

How kind.
Tell him I wish him joys of all varieties.

(Goes back inside.)

MASCARILLE

This man defies all manners and proprieties.
(He knocks.)
Please, sir: I've almost finished with my task.
There's an urgent favor that he'd like to ask.

ALBERT

I'm at his service, whenever he may call.

MASCARILLE

(Detaining him:)
Wait; two words more, and I'll have said it all.
He'd like to drop by briefly, and confer
With you upon a weighty matter, sir.

ALBERT

And what, if I may ask, is this affair
Which we must ponder?

MASCARILLE

He's just become aware
Of a great secret which, without a doubt,
Both of you will be much concerned about.
There: That's my message.

Scene 3

Albert.

ALBERT

Just Heaven! I quake with fear:
We seldom see each other; what brings him here?

My schemes, no doubt, are known; their doom is sealed.
This "secret's" one I dread to see revealed.
Someone's betrayed me in the hope of gain,
And now my honor bears a lasting stain.
My fraud's discovered. Alas, the cleverest crime
Can't hide the truth for any length of time,
And how much better for my name and soul
If I had let my conscience take control:
Its voice advised me twenty times and more
To give his rightful wealth to Polidore,
And, settling matters in a quiet way,
Avoid the shame which threatens me today.
But no, I've lost my chance; it's now too late.
The wealth that fraud brought into my estate
Must now depart from me, and once it's flown
I shall have lost a fair part of my own.

Scene 4

Albert, Polidore.

POLIDORE
(Saying the first four lines before seeing Albert:)
To wed in secret, letting no one know!
How will it end, if our children flout us so?
I wish I knew. And I fear the young girl's sire
Both for his wealth and his paternal ire.
But there he is.

ALBERT
Gods! Polidore draws near.

POLIDORE

I cannot face him.

ALBERT

I am held back by fear.

POLIDORE

How am I to begin?

ALBERT

What shall I say?

POLIDORE

He looks upset.

ALBERT

His face is drawn and gray.

POLIDORE

Judging by your expression, you're aware
Of what has brought me here, Monsieur Albert.

ALBERT

Alas, I am.

POLIDORE

Well may you crease your brow.
I couldn't believe what I was told just now.

ALBERT

I should be blushing for chagrin and shame.

POLIDORE

An action of the kind is much to blame,
And there is no excusing it, I hold.

ALBERT

God's merciful to sinners, we are told.

POLIDORE

What shall we be, then—merciful, or just?

ALBERT

We must be Christian.

POLIDORE

Yes indeed, we must.

ALBERT

In the name of God, forgive me, Polidore!

POLIDORE

That's what *I* ask. Forgive me, I implore.

ALBERT

Upon my knees I utter my appeal.

(Kneels.)

POLIDORE

What! *I*, not you, should be the one to kneel.

(Kneels.)

ALBERT

Look with some pity on my sorry case.

POLIDORE

I supplicate you in my deep disgrace.

ALBERT

The goodness of your heart amazes me.

POLIDORE

I'm overwhelmed by your humility.

ALBERT

Once more, forgive me!

POLIDORE

Pardon *me,* once more!

ALBERT

What has occurred I utterly deplore.

POLIDORE

Your grief could not be greater than my own.

ALBERT

I beg you not to let this thing be known.

POLIDORE

Monsieur Albert, I feel the same as you.

ALBERT

Preserve my honor.

POLIDORE

That, sir, I shall do.

ALBERT

Now, as for money, please say what you require.

POLIDORE

I ask no money; do as you desire.
In all such matters, I wish you to decide,
And if you're happy, I'll be satisfied.

ALBERT

How good you are! What godlike traits you show!

POLIDORE

You, too, are godlike, after such a blow!

ALBERT

May all go well with you, through Heaven's grace!

POLIDORE

God bless you!

ALBERT

Come; a brotherly embrace.

POLIDORE

With all my heart, and I am glad indeed
That we can end thus happily agreed.

ALBERT

Yes, thank the Lord.

(They rise from their knees.)

POLIDORE

When I learned, sir, what my son
And your Lucile had so unwisely done,
I frankly feared your anger, and expected
That you, so well-to-do and well connected . . .

59

ALBERT

What's this about Lucile, and being unwise?

POLIDORE

If that offends you, I'll apologize.
My son's done wrong, I'll readily admit,
And if it will relieve your grief a bit,
I'll even say that he *alone* did wrong;
That your daughter's virtue was too pure and strong
To let her go astray or gravely err,
Had not a wicked tempter prompted her;
That the villain took advantage of her trust
And so reduced your hopes for her to dust.
Yet since the thing is done, and since we find
Ourselves, thank Heaven, attuned in heart and mind,
Let's pardon all, and let all wrongs be righted
When, in the church, our children are united.

ALBERT

(*Aside:*)
So, I was wrong! But now this news! Perplexed,
I go from one great worry to the next,
And, doubly muddled, don't know what to say.
If I speak, I fear I'll give myself away.

POLIDORE

What's on your mind, sir?

ALBERT

Nothing. I think that I'll
Suspend our conversation for a while.
I suddenly feel sick, and must depart.

Scene 5

Polidore.

POLIDORE

I know his feelings, and can read his heart.
Reason has said to him *forgive, forget,*
But his deep anger's not appeased as yet.
His sense of wrong revives, and so he flees,
To hide from me his turmoil and unease.
His sorrow touches me, I share his grief.
Patience and time must bring his heart relief.
A woe too soon suppressed will but redouble.
Well, here's the foolish cause of all our trouble.

Scene 6

Polidore, Valère.

POLIDORE

So, my fine fellow! Your antics, it appears,
Will fill with grief your father's latter years;
Must I, each day, be forced to hear reports
Of freaks and follies of a hundred sorts?

VALÈRE

To what incessant crimes do you refer?
How have I earned my father's fury, sir?

POLIDORE

Ah, yes! I'm a strange man, and a testy one,
To criticize so wise and good a son!
Just look! His life is saintly, and he stays

At home all day upon his knees, and prays!
Has he ever twisted Nature's laws awry
By turning night to day? No, that's a lie!
Has he, in scores of cases, failed to show
Due deference to his father? Heavens, no!
And did he lately, in a secret rite,
Marry the daughter of Albert by night,
Reckless of consequences grave and bad?
No, that was someone else; this innocent lad
Has no idea of what those charges meant.
Wretch, sent by Heaven as my punishment,
Shall you be willful always? Shall not I
See you act wisely once before I die?

VALÈRE

(Alone:)
What caused this outburst? It appears to me
That the only answer could be Mascarille.
The rogue would never admit it. Therefore I'm
Forced to use trickery, and for a time
Conceal my anger.

Scene 7

Valère, Mascarille.

VALÈRE

   My father is aware,
Good Mascarille, of the secret which we share.

MASCARILLE

He is?

VALÈRE

Yes.

MASCARILLE

Who in the Devil let him know?

VALÈRE

I cannot guess who would betray us so.
Still, his reaction has amazed me quite,
And given me every reason for delight.
He showed no anger, and in a gentle voice
Forgave my trespass and approved my choice.
I wish I knew who's prompted him to be
So loving, and to show such leniency.
Someone has helped to lift my spirits high.

MASCARILLE

And what, sir, would you say if it were I
Who was the cause of your glad frame of mind?

VALÈRE

Come, come: Let's have no nonsense of that kind.

MASCARILLE

'Twas I, sir, I—as your father could relate—
Who brought about your present cheerful state.

VALÈRE

Truly? No jokes, now.

MASCARILLE

The Devil take me, sir,
If I'm a jester or a perjurer.

VALÈRE

(Drawing his sword:)
The Devil take me, too, if I do not
Give you your just deserts upon the spot!

MASCARILLE

Sir, I'm astonished. What would you kill me for?

VALÈRE

Is this the loyalty which once you swore?
If I hadn't tricked you, you'd never have confessed
To a guilty fact which I'd already guessed.
Those babbling lips of yours, which never tire,
Have brought on me the fury of my sire.
You've ruined me and, therefore, be prepared
To die.

MASCARILLE

No, no. Not yet. Let me be spared.
My soul's not ready for it. I beg you, wait
And see how all this will eventuate.
I had the best of reasons to reveal
A marriage you yourself could scarce conceal:
It was a master stroke, and you shall see
That you are wrong to be enraged at me.
What ground is there for anger, so long as through
My efforts all your wishes can come true,
And you be free of secrecy and strain?

VALÈRE

And what if all your talk proves false and vain?

MASCARILLE

Then you'll be free to kill me, as before.

But that won't happen. I have schemes galore,
And in the end you'll think me heaven-sent,
And thank me for my brilliant management.

VALÈRE

We'll see. Lucile, now . . .

MASCARILLE

Wait! Her father's here.

Scene 8

Albert, Valère, Mascarille.

ALBERT

(Saying the first five lines before seeing Valère:)
Recovering from my earlier shock and fear,
I marvel that so strange a tale misled
My anxious mind and filled my heart with dread.
Lucile assures me that there's nothing in it,
And I don't doubt her statement for a minute.
Ah, sir! Are you the brazen youth who glories
In slandering people with your untrue stories?

MASCARILLE

Monsieur Albert, don't fly into a passion.
Do treat your son-in-law in gentler fashion.

ALBERT

What son-in-law? Rascal, you look to me
Like the mainspring of some conspiracy
Of which you were the chief inventor, too.

MASCARILLE

I don't see what can be upsetting you.

ALBERT

You think it splendid, do you, to defame
My daughter, and besmirch our family name?

MASCARILLE

This gentleman is yours, sir, to command.

ALBERT

Let him tell the truth, then. That's my sole demand,
If he was partial to Lucile, he could
Have sought her hand as a proper suitor would;
That is, he could have been obedient
To custom, and applied for my consent,
Rather than be perverse, and give offense
To decency by this absurd pretense.

MASCARILLE

Pretense? Was Lucile not wedded secretly
To my master?

ALBERT

No, rogue, and she'll never be.

MASCARILLE

But if in fact a secret knot was tied,
Would you give your blessing to the groom and bride?

ALBERT

And if it's proved that there was no such wedding,
Would you rather die by hanging or beheading?

VALÈRE

Sir, if you'll let me, I can prove to you
That he's told the truth.

ALBERT

Well! Here's a master who
Deserves this flunky. Two liars in a row!

MASCARILLE

On my word of honor, what I say is so.

VALÈRE

Why should we wish to fool you, Monsieur Albert?

ALBERT

(Aside:)
They work together, like card sharks at a fair.

MASCARILLE

But come, let's cut this quarrel short, say I:
Bring out Lucile, and let her testify.

ALBERT

And what if she declares your tale untrue?

MASCARILLE

That, sir, is something that she cannot do.
Just promise to give their union your consent,
And I'll accept the direst punishment
If she does not confess to us a great
Love for my master and for her wedded state.

ALBERT

Well, we shall see.

(He goes and knocks on his door.)

MASCARILLE

(To Valère:)
    Don't worry. Be of good cheer.

ALBERT

Come out, Lucile!

VALÈRE

(To Mascarille:)
    I fear . . .

MASCARILLE

    Ah, never fear.

Scene 9

Lucile, Albert, Valère, Mascarille.

MASCARILLE

Monsieur Albert, be still, please. Madam, this
Is a moment which could bring you perfect bliss.
Your sire, informed now of your love, allows
Your choice of husband and approves your vows,
Provided that, unforced and unafraid,
You will confirm the statements we have made.

LUCILE

What is this saucy villain trying to say?

MASCARILLE

Good! We begin with compliments, right away.

LUCILE

Do tell me, sir; what clever brain created
This tale that's now so widely circulated?

VALÈRE

Forgive me; 'twas my man who dared reveal
The secret of our marriage, dear Lucile.

LUCILE

Our marriage?

VALÈRE

　　Yes, it's all come out, my dear,
And nothing can be hidden now, I fear.

LUCILE

So: Out of ardent love I've made you mine?

VALÈRE

All men must envy me a fate so fine:
Yet I ascribe my amorous success
Less to your ardor than to kindliness.
I know your temper must be sorely tried:
Our vows were something that you wished to hide,
And I have curbed all signs of rapture, lest
I violate the wish you had expressed.
But . . .

MASCARILLE

　　Yes, I did it; and what harm was done?

LUCILE

Was there ever a bolder falsehood under the sun?
You keep on lying, even to my face.

69

Do you think to gain me by a means so base?
Ah, what a noble lover! Because you lack
My love, it is my honor you attack,
In hopes that Father, shaken by your claim,
Will force on me a marriage full of shame!
No, even if all things were to take your part—
The Fates, my father, the wishes of my heart—
I'd still resist, with an indignant ire,
The Fates, my father, and my heart's desire,
And die before I married a complete
Scoundrel who sought to win me by deceit.
Enough, sir. If decorum did not ban
My sex from doing violence to a man,
I'd teach you what it means to treat me thus.

VALÈRE

(To Mascarille:)
Nothing will soothe her now. She's furious.

MASCARILLE

Sir, let me speak to her. Madam, if you please,
What is the point of these perversities?
What can you mean? What curious whim requires
That you take arms against your own desires?
If your sire were of the harsh, forbidding kind,
I'd understand; but he has an open mind,
And he has promised me that in confessing
Your secret to him, you shall gain his blessing.
No doubt 'twill make you feel a little shy
To admit the yearning you've been mastered by,
But if that flame now gives you sleepless nights,
A happy marriage will set all to rights;
And passion such as yours, though much decried,
Is not so grave a sin as homicide.

The flesh is weak, as men have always known,
And a girl, moreover, isn't made of stone.
You're not the first, as the old saying goes,
And you won't be the last one, Heaven knows.

LUCILE

Can you listen, Father, to such words as these,
And not reprove their gross indignities?

ALBERT

What would you have me say, dear? I'm afraid
Rage makes me speechless.

MASCARILLE

Madam, you should have made
A frank confession, and so closed the case.

LUCILE

What is there to confess?

MASCARILLE

Why, what took place
Between my master and you! You're teasing me.

LUCILE

And what, you monster of effrontery,
Took place between your master and me?

MASCARILLE

You ought
To know far better than I, I should have thought,
And you cannot have forgotten the delight
Which you experienced on a certain night.

LUCILE

Father, this lackey has forgot his place.

(She gives Mascarille a slap in the face.)

Scene 10

Albert, Valère, Mascarille.

MASCARILLE

I do believe she's slapped me in the face.

ALBERT

Begone, you villain. What she did, by God,
I, as her father, heartily applaud.

MASCARILLE

Nevertheless, if anything I've said
Was not the truth, may Heaven strike me dead.

ALBERT

Nevertheless, may both my ears be cropped
If your brash chatter isn't quickly stopped.

MASCARILLE

Shall I bring two witnesses who'll prove me true?

ALBERT

Shall I call two men to whack and cudgel you?

MASCARILLE

They'll validate my story, every bit.

ALBERT

Their brawn will make up for my lack of it.

MASCARILLE

Lucile behaved so out of bashfulness.

ALBERT

For *your* behavior I shall have redress.

MASCARILLE

Do you know Ormin? He's that notary, plump and witty.

ALBERT

Do you know Grimpant, the hangman of this city?

MASCARILLE

And Simon the tailor, renowned for formal wear?

ALBERT

And the gallows tree, set up in the market square?

MASCARILLE

Those two were good friends of the bride and groom.

ALBERT

Those two will drag you off to meet your doom.

MASCARILLE

For witnesses, the couple chose those two.

ALBERT

Those two will witness my revenge on you.

73

MASCARILLE

They saw the nuptials of the happy pair.

ALBERT

And they shall see you dancing in the air.

MASCARILLE

A black veil hid the features of the bride.

ALBERT

They'll hoist the black flag for you, once you've died.

MASCARILLE

You old, pig-headed man!

ALBERT

Accursèd faker!
I'm old, and you had better thank your Maker
That I can't repay your insolence just now.
But I shall, don't worry. That's my solemn vow.

Scene 11

Valère, Mascarílle.

VALÈRE

Well, well: The happy outcome that you planned . . .

MASCARILLE

No need to say it, sir; I understand:
All's turned against me; on all sides I see
Cudgels and swords and gallows threatening me.
I shall escape this nightmare only if

I hurl myself head foremost from a cliff,
And that's what I shall do, so long as I
Can find a cliff that's adequately high.
Farewell, sir.

VALÈRE

No, no; don't you try to flee.
Your death is something that I want to see.

MASCARILLE

I cannot die, sir, under someone's eyes.
You force me to postpone my sad demise.

VALÈRE

Come, lest my vexed belovèd make you pay
For the insults you have given her today.

MASCARILLE

(Alone:)
Poor Mascarille, what worries and chagrins
Are heaped on you through other people's sins!

Act Four

Scene 1

Ascagne, Frosine.

FROSINE

It's a troubling turn of events.

ASCAGNE

        Frosine, dear friend,
Fate has decreed for me a dismal end.
Things have now gone so far, in this affair,
That matters can't conceivably stop there;
Lucile, and my Valère, astonished by
These late events, will seek to clarify
The mystery which made them disagree,
And that will ruin both my schemes and me.
For—whether Albert was privy to deceit
Or taken in, like others, by the cheat—

If ever the truth about me should be known,
And all that wealth he's added to his own
Be taken away, think how he'd then regard me!
Unless I bring him wealth, he will discard me.
No more affection. And however my
Imposture looked then to my lover's eye,
Would he respect a wife who could not claim
A fortune, and who had no family name?

FROSINE

That is a clear and cool analysis,
But you should have made it earlier than this.
What hid the truth from you until this hour?
One didn't have to have prophetic power
To see, when first you schemed to catch Valère,
The risks of which you've now become aware.
'Twas in the cards; from the start I've understood
That your trickery couldn't come to any good.

ASCAGNE

I'm desperate, Frosine. Pretend that you
Are in my place, and tell me what to do.

FROSINE

If I put myself in your place, it will be
Your office, then, to lend advice to me,
For I shall then be you, and you'll be I:
"Frosine, you see how all has gone awry;
Tell me, I pray, what steps I ought to take."

ASCAGNE

Oh, don't make fun of me, for mercy's sake!
It's wrong of you, when I am so distressed,
To treat my situation as a jest.

FROSINE

I share your heartsick feelings, rest assured,
And I'd give anything to see them cured.
But what can I do? Alas, I don't see how
Your amorous wishes can be furthered now.

ASCAGNE

If there's no hope for me, then I must die.

FROSINE

Don't hurry, please, to bid the world good-bye.
Death's a fine remedy, but it's the sort
One should use only as a last resort.

ASCAGNE

Frosine, I mean it: If I cannot be led,
By your kind help, through all that looms ahead,
I'll let despair possess me altogether.

FROSINE

I've just now thought of something. I wonder whether . . .
But here's Éraste, who might disrupt our talk.
Let us discuss this matter while we walk.
Come, come, let's vanish.

Scene 2

Éraste, Gros-René.

ÉRASTE

So. Rebuffed once more?

GROS-RENÉ

There never was, sir, an ambassador
So coldly treated. I'd hardly said how you
Hoped that she'd grant a moment's interview,
When she broke in and in a haughty style
Said, "Go! Both you and he are low and vile.
Tell him to keep his distance." Having sent
That charming message, she turned her back and went.
Then Marinette got on her high horse, too,
And said to me, "Be off, you lackey, you,"
And left me standing there. Your luck and mine
Are much the same: We're no one's valentine.

ÉRASTE

The thankless woman! To scorn a heart which for
Good cause was vexed, yet now is hers once more!
What! If it seems his trust has been abused,
Ought not a lover's rage to be excused?
And could my heart, at that dark moment, be
Indifferent to a rival's victory?
Who wouldn't have raged like me, as things then were,
Loath though I was to think the worst of her?
Was I slow to set aside my just suspicions?
Did I trouble her for oaths and depositions?
No; at a time when all is still unsure,
I raise to her a worship deep and pure,
And ask her pardon. Yet she makes little of
My homage, and the grandeur of my love.
Alas, she will not cure my heart of quaking
With fears and envies of my rival's making;
She dooms me to be jealous, and dares refuse
All notes, all messages, all interviews!
Clearly her love was never very strong
If it could die of such a trivial wrong;

In her abrupt severity I see
Too plainly what, in truth, she feels for me,
And just how highly I should now esteem
Those flighty charms which led my heart to dream.
No, I'll no more be at the beck and call
Of one whose feeling for me is so small;
And since she can so coldly spurn her lover,
I'll do the same, and be unburdened of her.

GROS-RENÉ

I'll do that, too, sir. Let our loves be classed
With ancient sins, and errors of the past.
Let's teach those fickle women to behave,
And let them know that we're still tough and brave.
If a man's afraid of hens, then he'll be pecked.
If men were only to demand respect,
The women wouldn't talk so big and loud.
It's our own fault that they've become so proud:
I'm hanged if I don't think that all their sex
Would soon be shyly clinging to our necks
If it were not for all the silly ways
That most men spoil the creatures nowadays.

ÉRASTE

For me, disdain's a thing that can't be borne;
And I propose to match her scorn for scorn
By giving my affection to another.

GROS-RENÉ

For me, a woman isn't worth the bother;
I shall renounce them all, and it's my view
That you'd do well to do without them, too.
For, sir, a woman is, without a doubt,
An animal that's hard to figure out,

81

Whose nature has been wicked since the Fall:
And since an animal's an animal,
And never shall be otherwise, although
It live a hundred thousand years, just so
Woman is always woman, and shall stay
A woman even to the Judgment Day.
Whence a wise Greek observed that woman's head
Is like a quicksand. Listen to what he said
In this most cogent train of reasoning:
Just as the head is like the body's king,
And the body without the king becomes a brute,
If the king and the head get into a dispute,
So that the compass wavers from its course,
Certain confusions then arise, perforce;
The brutal part would gain the mastery
Over the rational; the one cries "gee,"
The other, "haw"; the one would have it slow,
The other fast, and all is touch and go.
Which goes to show, interpreters explain,
That a woman's head is like a weathervane
Up on the roof, which the least breeze can turn;
And that's why Aristotle, as we learn,
Said women are like the sea, a thought which gave
Our tongue the saying, "steady as a wave."
So, by comparison (for comparing brings
A vividness into our reasonings,
And scholars like myself prefer a shrewd
Comparison to a mere similitude):
Well, by comparison, Master, if I may:
As when the sea is stormy, and the spray
Begins to fly, the winds to shriek and squall,
Waves to collide and make a dreadful brawl,
And the ship, for all the steersman's art, is tossed
Twixt cellar and attic, and is all but lost,

So, when a woman lets that head of hers
Fill up with wild ideas, a storm occurs
In which the witch opinionates and raves,
Until the . . . tide, you know . . . or else the waves . . .
Or, so to speak, a sandbar . . . or a reef . . .
Oh, women are nothing but a lot of grief.

ÉRASTE

Well argued.

GROS-RENÉ

  It wasn't bad, I'm glad to say.
But look, I see the two of them bound this way.
Stand firm, sir.

ÉRASTE

  Don't you worry.

GROS-RENÉ

  I fear that her
Bright eyes may once more take you prisoner.

Scene 3

Lucile, Éraste, Marinette, Gros-René.

MARINETTE

I see that he's still here; now, don't relent.

LUCILE

Don't worry; I'm not weak to that extent.

MARINETTE

He's coming towards us.

ÉRASTE

No, no, madam, I'm
Not here to court you yet another time.
That's over; my heart is healing, and I now see
How little of your own you gave to me.
Your lasting anger at my slight offense
Shows all too clearly your indifference;
And scorn, as I shall make you well aware,
Is what a noble spirit cannot bear.
I once discovered in your eyes, I own,
A charm and beauty which were yours alone,
And, as your ardent slave, preferred my chain
To any scepter that I might obtain.
Yes, I adored you in the deepest way;
You were my life; and I am forced to say
That after all, however much offended,
I'll find it painful that my suit is ended,
That my hurt soul, though it intends to heal,
May bleed a long time from the wound I feel,
And that, though freed from a yoke I gladly bore,
It must resolve itself to love no more.
But what's the good of talking? Since you decline
So hatefully each overture of mine,
This is the last time I shall trouble you
With the anguished feelings I am going through.

LUCILE

As for *my* feelings, sir, I'd be elated
If this last speech of yours were terminated.

ÉRASTE

Well then, my lady, cross me off your list!
I'll break with you forever, as you insist;

Yes, yes, I'll break with you, and I shan't try
To speak with you again; I'd rather die.

LUCILE

So much the better.

ÉRASTE

No, no, you'd be wrong
To think that I'll back down. Though I'm not strong
Enough to bar your image from my heart,
Yet I assure you now that, when we part,
I shan't come back.

LUCILE

To do so would be vain.

ÉRASTE

I'd hack myself to bits before I'd deign
To stoop so low as to revisit one
Who'd so mistreated me as you have done.

LUCILE

So be it. Let's say no more about it.

ÉRASTE

Yes,
Let's put an end to all this wordiness,
And let me give you solid proof that I've
Determined to escape your toils alive.
I shall keep nothing by me which could set
My heart to mourning what it must forget.
Here is your portrait: It delights the eye
With all the charms you are attended by,

85

And yet they hide a hundred faults from view:
It's an impostor I return to you.

GROS-RENÉ

Good!

LUCILE

Since you are returning everything,
I'll do the same: Take back your diamond ring.

MARINETTE

Well done!

ÉRASTE

This lock of hair is yours once more.

LUCILE

Your agate seal I hasten to restore.

ÉRASTE

(Reading:)
"You say your love is limitless, Éraste.
Though I'm not sure that mine is quite so vast,
    This I can say with certainty:
    I love it that Éraste loves me.
            Lucile"
Those warm words gave me leave to pay you court,
But you deceived me. This is my retort.

(He tears up the letter.)

LUCILE

(Reading:)
"I don't know what will be my passion's fate,
Or for how long my longing heart must wait;

But I know this—that I shall feel
Eternal love for you, Lucile.
                    Éraste"
This says you'll love me through eternity.
You and this letter both have lied to me.

(She tears up the letter.)

                    GROS-RENÉ

Go on.

                    ÉRASTE

(Tearing up a letter:)
    This one's from you. It, too, shall go.

                    MARINETTE

(To Lucile:)
Steady.

                    LUCILE

And so shall these, I'll have him know.

                    GROS-RENÉ

(To Éraste:)
Be firm. Resist her.

                    MARINETTE

(To Lucile:)
    Don't break down. Stand fast.

                    LUCILE

(Tearing up letters:)
Here go the rest.

ÉRASTE

Thank Heaven! Free at last!
May I die, if I go back on what I said!

LUCILE

If I break my word, may Heaven strike me dead!

ÉRASTE

Farewell, then.

LUCILE

Yes, farewell.

MARINETTE

(To Lucile:)

You did just right.

GROS-RENÉ

(To Éraste:)
You got the best of it.

MARINETTE

(To Lucile:)

Let's get out of sight.

GROS-RENÉ

(To Éraste:)
You've battled bravely; now you must come away.

MARINETTE

(To Lucile:)
Why are you waiting?

GROS-RENÉ

(To Éraste:)
    Why must you delay?

ÉRASTE

Lucile, Lucile, I know you'll grieve and pine,
Remembering that you lost a heart like mine.

LUCILE

Éraste, Éraste, a heart like yours is found
Quite easily; one has but to look around.

ÉRASTE

No, no, search everywhere and you'll find none
That could adore you as my heart has done.
I don't speak now in hopes that you'll relent:
In such a cause, my words would be misspent.
All my devotion could not move or win you;
You broke with me; my hopes cannot continue.
But after me, though others swoon and sigh,
None will so truly cherish you as I.

LUCILE

When we love someone, we treat that person kindly,
And never would accuse that person blindly.

ÉRASTE

When we love someone, appearances may be
Conducive to a fit of jealousy,
But a true lover could not send away
The one she loves, as you have done today.

LUCILE

Jealousy need not slander and abuse.

ÉRASTE

A passionate error's easy to excuse.

LUCILE

Ah no, Éraste, you do not truly love me.

ÉRASTE

Lucile, you've never been enamored of me.

LUCILE

Ha! I don't think that greatly troubles you.
Perhaps the wisest thing for me to do
Was never . . . But let us drop this idle chatter:
I've nothing more to say about the matter.

ÉRASTE

Why not?

LUCILE

Because we two are separating,
And have no time for bickering and debating.

ÉRASTE

We're parting?

LUCILE

Yes: Is there any cause to doubt it?

ÉRASTE

How can you sound so matter-of-fact about it?

LUCILE

You sound the same.

ÉRASTE

I?

LUCILE

Yes; one hates to show
How much it hurts to let somebody go.

ÉRASTE

But, cruel one, 'twas you who wanted it,

LUCILE

I? Not at all. 'Twas you, you must admit.

ÉRASTE

I thought you'd be made happy by the break.

LUCILE

Not so. You wished it for your own sweet sake.

ÉRASTE

But what if, yearning for captivity,
My sad heart begged you now to pardon me?

LUCILE

No, no, you mustn't: I'm weak, and I'm afraid
I'd grant too quickly the request you made.

ÉRASTE

Ah, no! You could not pardon me too soon,
Or I too quickly ask you for that boon:
Pray grant it, madam; this great love of mine
Must never cease to worship at your shrine.
Again I ask it; will you not confer
Your gracious pardon?

LUCILE

Take me home now, sir.

Scene 4

Marinette, Gros-René.

MARINETTE

Oh, the spineless creature!

GROS-RENÉ

What a craven quitter.

MARINETTE

I blush for her.

GROS-RENÉ

I'm furious and bitter.
Don't think that I'll give in to you that way.

MARINETTE

You won't fool me like that, try as you may.

GROS-RENÉ

Don't stir me up, or I'll go through the ceiling.

MARINETTE

Remember who I am, now; you're not dealing
With my foolish mistress. Look at that pretty mug!
My, how it makes me want to kiss him. Ugh!
Do you think I'd fall in love with such a face,
And let myself be squeezed in your embrace—
A girl like me?

GROS-RENÉ

We're quits then, it appears.
Well, not to hem and haw about it, here's
The cap you gave me, with its plume of red.
It will no longer crown my noble head.

MARINETTE

To show my scorn for you in the same way,
Here is that paper of pins which yesterday
You gave me with a philanthropic air.

GROS-RENÉ

Take back your knife; it's an object rich and rare.
It must have cost you twenty cents, that's plain.

MARINETTE

Take back your scissors and their copper chain.

GROS-RENÉ

Here's that piece of cheese you gave me. If I could
Give back the soup you gave me then, I would,
For then I'd owe you not a thing, my dear.

MARINETTE

I don't have all your letters with me here,
But when they burn, they'll make a lovely flame.

GROS-RENÉ

And what do you think I'll do with yours? The same.

MARINETTE

Do you think I'm going to take you back? No, never!

GROS-RENÉ

(*Picking up a straw:*)
The way to stay unreconciled forever
Is to break a straw in two, for it's a token
Of separation when a straw is broken.
Now, don't make eyes. I want to be irate.

MARINETTE

Don't wink at me. I'm in a furious state.

GROS-RENÉ

Come, break the straw now, so we can't back down.
You witch, you're laughing!

MARINETTE

You made me laugh, you clown.

GROS-RENÉ

Plague take your laughing: My rage has all abated.
Well, what do you say? Shall we be separated,
Or shall we not?

MARINETTE

You say.

GROS-RENÉ

You say.

MARINETTE

No, you.

GROS-RENÉ

Shall there be no more love between us two?

MARINETTE

Just as you wish.

GROS-RENÉ

What's *your* wish? Don't be shy.

MARINETTE

I shall say nothing.

GROS-RENÉ

Neither shall I.

MARINETTE

Nor I.

GROS-RENÉ

Oh, let's stop all this nonsense, for Heaven's sake.
Shake hands; I pardon you.

MARINETTE

I forgive you. Shake.

GROS-RENÉ

My, how she charms me! More than I can say!

MARINETTE

How Marinette adores her Gros-René!

Act Five

———⟡———

Scene 1

Mascarille.

MASCARILLE

"When darkness falls," he said, "I mean to steal
Into the residence of my dear Lucile.
Go home now, and make ready with great speed
Some arms, and the dark lantern we shall need."
When he said those words, I felt as if he'd said,
"Get ready to be hanged until you're dead."
Come now, my Master; because your order sent
Me reeling backwards in astonishment,
I hadn't time to question or debate;
But now I wish to speak, and set you straight:
Defend yourself; let's reason equably.
You wish, you say, to go tonight and see
Lucile? "Yes, Mascarille." What shall you do?

"What a true lover is expected to."
What a true idiot would do, who takes
A needless risk, and plays for mortal stakes.
"But you know what my motive is, my spur:
Lucile is angry." So much the worse for her.
"But love has bade me soothe her troubled heart."
But love's an ass; he isn't very smart.
If we met an angry brother, sire or rival,
Just how would love assure us of survival?
"Do you think that any of those would cause a brawl?"
Indeed I do; your rival, most of all.
"Don't worry, Mascarille; we'll go well armed,
And if we're challenged we shall not be harmed;
We'll fight them off." We will? That's just the sort
Of thing I don't regard as healthy sport.
I, fight? Good Lord! Am I some Roland, then,
Or some Achilles? Master, think again.
When I, who hold myself so dear, reflect
That an inch or two of steel can so affect
The body as to put one in the grave,
I'm shocked, and feel no impulse to be brave.
"But you'll be armored, head to foot." Then I'd
Be heavy, and couldn't run away and hide.
And furthermore, there's always some loose joint
Through which a sword can thrust its wicked point.
"They'll call you a coward." I don't care if they do,
So long as I can move my jaws and chew.
At table I can do the work of four,
But I'm a zero, sir, in fight or war.
Though the other world may seem to you a treat,
I find the air of this one very sweet,
And death's a thing that I'm not wild about.
If you choose to play the fool, just count me out.

Scene 2

Valère, Mascarille.

VALÈRE

I've never lived through such a tedious day.
The sun in Heaven seems to stay and stay,
And has so long a course to cover yet
Before it can pull in its rays and set,
I doubt its journey ever will be done.
It maddens me, the slowness of the sun.

MASCARILLE

Why yearn to plunge into the dark, intent
On figuring in some gruesome incident? . . .
Lucile's rebuffs have been both firm and plain . . .

VALÈRE

Spare me such talk. It's bothersome and vain.
I'd fight a hundred foes, could I appease
Her wrath, which has my soul in agonies;
And if I cannot melt her heart, I'll die.
My mind's made up.

MASCARILLE

    Sir, we see eye to eye.
But when we go in there, shouldn't we be
Unnoticed?

VALÈRE

    Yes.

MASCARILLE

    Then something worries me.

VALÈRE

What's that?

MASCARILLE

I have a most tormenting cough,
The sound of which could tip their servants off.
(*He coughs.*)
I've never had a cough so bad as this.

VALÈRE

Well, it will pass. Just chew some licorice.

MASCARILLE

I don't believe, sir, that this cough will pass.
I wish I could go with you but, alas,
Think what regret I'd suffer if it were
My fault that something happened to you, sir.

Scene 3

Valère, La Rapière, Mascarille.

LA RAPIÈRE

I've just had word, sir, from an honest source
That Èraste's enraged, and may resort to force;
Meanwhile, Albert declares that he will slaughter
Your Mascarille for slandering his daughter.

MASCARILLE

I? I? All this has nothing to do with me.
Do I deserve this talk of butchery?
Am I in charge of the virginities
Of all the girls in town? Just tell me, please:

Can I prevent temptation? And if they
Give in to it, what can I do or say?

VALÈRE

(To La Rapière:)
Our foes are not so fierce as you've been told;
And, though his passion may have made him bold,
Éraste will find that scaring us is hard.

LA RAPIÈRE

If you have need, sir, of a bodyguard,
I'll serve you in all weathers, foul or fair.

VALÈRE

You're kind to offer me such aid and care.

LA RAPIÈRE

I have two friends I'll bring you if I can,
Tough fellows who will draw on any man,
And who could guarantee your peace of mind.

MASCARILLE

We'd better hire them, sir.

VALÈRE

Sir, you're too kind.

LA RAPIÈRE

And little Gille, as well, could lend his aid,
But for the fatal slip he lately made.
What a shame! An able man! Perhaps you saw
What a scurvy trick was played him by the law;
He died like Caesar. Breaking him on the wheel,
The executioner couldn't make him squeal.

VALÈRE

A man like that is a great loss, indeed;
But as for your good offer, we shall not need
Protection.

LA RAPIÈRE

As you like, but don't forget
That he's looking for you, and may find you yet.

VALÈRE

Well, just to prove to you that I'm undaunted,
If it's me he wants, I'll give him what is wanted.
I'll walk all through this town with fearless stride,
And none but this one servant at my side.

MASCARILLE

Oh, sir, you're tempting Heaven: How rash of you!
You know what threats are made against us two.
Oh!

VALÈRE

What are you looking at? Something sinister?

MASCARILLE

I smell a cudgel in the offing, sir.
But now, I beg you, let us be discreet
And not stand obstinately in the street;
Let's hide somewhere.

VALÈRE

Hide? Can you to my face
Propose—you knave!—that I do a thing so base?
Follow me now, and no more jabbering.

MASCARILLE

Dear Master, living is a lovely thing!
We have but one death, and it lasts so long! . . .

VALÈRE

If you speak again, I'll beat you like a gong.
Ascagne is coming. It's not yet clear to me
What side he takes in all this enmity.
Meanwhile, we shall go home and get our gear
For tonight's brave venture.

MASCARILLE

All I feel is fear.
A plague on love, and on these girls who taste
Love's fruit, and then act militantly chaste!

Scene 4

Ascagne, Frosine.

ASCAGNE

Then it's true, Frosine, all true beyond a doubt?
Pray tell the story, leaving nothing out.

FROSINE

You shall in time know all the facts, don't worry—
Since, as a rule, so wonderful a story
Is told, retold, and then repeated still.
All you need know is this: After that will
Had specified a male child as its heir,
Albert's wife was so luckless as to bear
A girl child. You, my dear. Albert then spun
A sly plot, taking as his own the son

Of Ignès the flower girl, who in reverse
Took you, and placed you in our house to nurse.
Some ten months later, when the boy fell prey
To a fatal chill, Albert being then away,
His wife, too, hatched a plot, by reason of
Her husband's temper and her mother love.
She took you back in secret then, to be
Once more a member of your family,
Her absent husband being notified
That his daughter, not his borrowed son, had died.
So! There's the secret of your birth revealed,
Which your feigned mother had till now concealed;
For that she's given her reasons, though I've guessed
That some weren't wholly in your interest.
In any case, my talk with her has brought
More blessings than we ever could have thought.
Ignès no longer claims you; thanks to Valère,
The time has come to lay your secret bare,
And she and I have let your father know
What his wife's diary proves to have been so;
Then, pressing our persuasions farther yet,
We've had the luck and cleverness to get
Albert and Polidore into a mood
Of tolerance, and a pliant attitude,
Telling the latter all these strange events
So gently that he did not take offense,
And, step by step, so leading him at last
To make adjustments and forgive the past
That he is quite as eager as your sire
To see you wed the husband you desire.

ASCAGNE

Frosine, my dear, what joy your words beget . . .
For all you've done, how great must be my debt!

FROSINE

One last thing: Polidore's in the mood for fun,
And bids us to say nothing to his son.

Scene 5

Polidore, Ascagne, Frosine.

POLIDORE

Come, Daughter, as I may call you now; for I
Now know the secret that your clothes belie.
You've done a daring deed, in which I find
Such spirit and such cleverness of mind,
I know how much my dear son will rejoice
When he finds out who's the lady of his choice.
He'll treasure you, and I shall do the same.
But here he comes; let's play a little game.
Go bring your people here.

ASCAGNE

　　　Sir, I'll obey you,
As a sign of that respect I'll always pay you.

Scene 6

Polidore, Valère, Mascarille.

MASCARILLE

(To Valère:)
Heaven sometimes warns us of an ill-starred thing.
I dreamt last night, sir, of a broken string
Of pearls, and broken eggs. Dark omens, eh?

VALÈRE

Coward!

POLIDORE

Valère, you face a test today
Where all your courage will be necessary.
Prepare to meet a potent adversary.

MASCARILLE

Will no one intervene, sir, and prevent
These foes from mutual dismemberment?
It's not my place to do so; but if through
Some dreadful chance your son is lost to you,
Don't blame me for it.

POLIDORE

No, no; in this case
I urge my son to face what he must face.

MASCARILLE

Unnatural father!

VALÈRE

Sir, in those words I hear
A brave man speaking, and one whom I revere.
I know that I've offended you; I repent
Of all I've done without your wise consent.
And yet, however angry you might be,
You've never ceased to hope the best of me,
And you do well to urge me not to let
Éraste's ill-tempered challenge go unmet.

POLIDORE

I worried about his anger until lately,
But now the state of things has altered greatly;

A stronger foe, from whom you cannot fly,
Will soon attack you.

MASCARILLE

Why all this fighting? Why?

VALÈRE

I fly, sir? God forbid. But who is my foe?

POLIDORE

Ascagne.

VALÈRE

Ascagne?

POLIDORE

He'll soon be here, I know.

VALÈRE

Strange! His good will toward me was so intense.

POLIDORE

Yes, it is he to whom you've given offense.
He asks you to the field of honor, where
In single fight you'll settle the affair.

MASCARILLE

He's a sterling man, who knows it's wrong to make
Others risk dying for his quarrel's sake.

POLIDORE

They charge you with imposture, and I have found
Their anger understandable and sound.
Albert and I, moreover, are agreed

That you must face Ascagne for that misdeed—
Both publicly, and promptly, if you please,
And with the usual formalities.

VALÈRE

How, Father, can Lucile continue to . . . ?

POLIDORE

She's marrying Éraste, and says that you
Have slandered her; and to disprove your lies,
She wants to say her vows before your eyes.

VALÈRE

Good God, what shamelessness, what impudence!
Can she have lost all honor, faith and sense?

Scene 7

Albert, Polidore, Lucile, Éraste, Valère, Mascarille.

ALBERT

Well, time for combat! Our man is close behind.
Have you got yours in a fighting frame of mind?

VALÈRE

Yes, yes, I'm ready, since you'd have me fight,
And if my wrath, at first, was slow to ignite,
A lingering devotion made it so,
And not the strength and valor of my foe;
But this, now, is too much; I feel no more
Devotion, and my thoughts are full of gore,
Faced as I am with perfidy so great
That my heart hungers to retaliate.

(To Lucile:)
Not that my heart desires you, at this stage:
All of its fires have changed to burning rage,
And once I've told the world your infamy,
Your guilty marriage will not trouble me.
What you intend, Lucile, is odious;
I can't believe it; I'm incredulous;
You are the enemy of your own good name,
And ought to perish of so great a shame.

LUCILE

Such harsh words would be staggering to hear,
If my avenger were not drawing near.
But here's Ascagne, who'll have the pleasure soon
Of teaching you to sing another tune;
It won't be hard.

Scene 8

Albert, Polidore, Ascagne, Lucile, Éraste, Valère, Frosine, Marinette, Gros-René, Mascarille.

VALÈRE

    He couldn't bully me
If he had a hundred arms. Too bad that he
Must risk his life for a guilty sister's sake,
But since he's made so foolish a mistake,
I'll meet his challenge—and yours, too, valiant friend.

ÉRASTE

A while ago, I was enraged no end,
But since Ascagne challenges you thus,
I'll step aside, and let him fight for us.

VALÈRE

That is, no doubt, a wise and prudent action.
But . . .

ÉRASTE

Rest assured, he'll give you satisfaction.

VALÈRE

He?

POLIDORE

Don't be hasty, now. You don't yet know
What a rare lad Ascagne is.

ALBERT

That's so,
And so Ascagne will show him presently.

VALÈRE

All right then, let him show me, let us see.

MARINETTE

In front of everyone?

GROS-RENÉ

It wouldn't be right.

VALÈRE

Are you making fun of me? By God, I'll smite
Whoever dares to laugh. Now, draw your blade.

ASCAGNE

No, no, I'm not so fierce as I'm portrayed;
In this encounter, which concerns all here,

It is my weakness that you'll meet, I fear.
You'll learn that Heaven did not bestow on me
A heart that could resist you, and you'll see
That destiny has chosen you to deal
A death blow to the brother of Lucile.
Yes, far from fighting what the Fates have planned,
Ascagne now must perish by your hand,
And shall be glad to breathe his last, if through
That sacrifice he can bring joy to you,
And, here and now, afford you as your own
A wife who must by law be yours alone.

                        VALÈRE
No, I shall never, after such treacheries
And shameless acts . . .

                       ASCAGNE
        Oh! Listen to me, please:
The heart that's pledged to you could not, Valère,
Have done you any wrong; to that I'll swear;
Its love is pure, its constancy entire.
I call, as witness to these things, your sire.

                       POLIDORE
Yes, Son, we've laughed enough at your vexation,
And now it's time you had an explanation.
The one you're pledged to, and your heart's desire,
Stands now before you, concealed in man's attire.
From childhood on, financial reasons made
Her family clothe her thus in masquerade,
And Love, of late, disguised her otherwise,
To trick you and conjoin our family ties.
Don't look around in shock at everyone;
What I have said is serious, my son.

Behold her who, by night, contrived to steal
Your vows, pretending that she was Lucile,
And who, by that contrivance, made us fall
Into a great confusion, one and all.
But now Ascagne shall change to Dorothée,
Your loves shall come into the light of day
And be confirmed now by a holier bond.

ALBERT

That sort of single combat, warm and fond,
Will satisfy us; and that's as well, because
The other kind's forbidden by our laws.

POLIDORE

I know that your bewilderment is great,
But in this matter you cannot hesitate.

VALÈRE

Ah, no, I wouldn't dream of such a thing;
And if this outcome is astonishing,
I relish the surprise, sir. I am seized
By love and wonder, and immensely pleased:
Can it be that those eyes . . .

ALBERT

Her clothes, Valère,
Don't suit the tender thoughts you'll soon declare.
Let's let her go and change, and meanwhile you
May learn your wife's whole story hitherto.

VALÈRE

Lucile, I was mistaken; forgive me, please.

LUCILE

Your angry words I can forget with ease.

ALBERT

Come, children; further friendly words can wait.
Let's all go to my house and celebrate.

ÉRASTE

But, sir, you have forgotten that there's still
A chance to see two warriors hack and kill.
Valère and I have found our mates today,
But what of Mascarille and Gros-René?
Which one of them shall win our Marinette?
That won't be settled till some blood is let.

MASCARILLE

My blood's inside me where it likes to be,
And he can marry her, for all of me.
I know her nature, and I can assert
That marriage vows won't make her cease to flirt.

MARINETTE

You think I'd take you for a lover? No.
A husband needn't be a Romeo;
He can be plain and dull and everyday.
But a lover ought to take one's breath away.

GROS-RENÉ

See here; I want you, once we're made one flesh,
To pay no heed when pretty boys get fresh.

MASCARILLE

You'll have her all to yourself, eh? Are you sure?

GROS-RENÉ

I am; I want a wife who's strict and pure,
Or I'll raise the Devil.

113

MASCARILLE

Ah, my boy, you'll soften,
As I've seen other husbands do so often.
Before they marry, they're rigid and severe,
But they get meek and tame within a year.

MARINETTE

Dear spouse, don't question my fidelity!
Sweet talkers won't get anywhere with me:
I'll tell you everything.

MASCARILLE

How nice, to make
One's spouse a confidant!

MARINETTE

Be still, you snake!

ALBERT

Once more, friends, let's go home and at our ease
Continue these most pleasant colloquies.

END OF PLAY

An Interview with the Translator

By Dana Gioia

No major American poet today has had a longer or closer relationship with theater than Richard Wilbur. He has been active in the field for six decades—ever since his translation of Molière's *Misanthrope* opened in 1955 at the legendary Poets' Theatre in Cambridge, Massachusetts. But Wilbur's sustained and prolific involvement in theater has been unusual. He has not written plays, not even verse drama. All of Wilbur's theatrical works, with the notable exception of lyrics for one Broadway musical—Leonard Bernstein's *Candide*—have been translations of classical French theater, especially the comedies of Molière.

The son of a painter, Wilbur was born in New York City in 1921 but was raised in rural New Jersey. He attended Amherst, where he chaired the college newspaper—an activity that seems typical for a future writer—but he also spent two summers riding the rails in Depression-era America. Graduating in 1942 as America entered World War II, Wilbur married his college sweetheart Charlotte Ward and joined the U.S. Army. He initially trained as a cryptographer, but his leftist associations led the army to transfer him to infantry. For the next three years he experienced some of the war's most brutal combat, from the Allied landing on the beaches of Italy to the final push into Germany. He often read in the lulls between battles and once even wrote a poem in a foxhole.

After the war Wilbur started graduate school at Harvard, where he became friends with Robert Frost. Wilbur had written poems since childhood, but the aspiring scholar now began working on them seriously. His literary success was almost immediate. He was from the first a natural poet with a distinctive and powerful personal style. With the publication of his first two books, *The Beautiful Changes* (1947) and *Ceremony* (1950), Wilbur was recognized as one of the finest poets of his generation, a judgment that has never been seriously challenged. Even his occasional detractors recognize his abundant talent; their complaint is only that he has not been sufficiently ambitious in exploring it. His champions have no hesitation in acclaiming him one of the major American poets of his age.

Awards came early in his career and have never stopped. Wilbur is the only living American poet to have won the Pulitzer Prize twice. He has also been awarded both the National Book Award and the Bollingen Prize, and he served as U.S. Poet Laureate.

Wilbur's work is elegantly formal and deeply intelligent— two literary qualities that in a lesser talent might undercut the poetry's emotional immediacy or lyric force. But Wilbur's language is so fresh and sensuously alive that his poems never seem stiff or preordained. He has the lyric poet's irreplaceable gift of bringing the reader directly into an experience in all its heady complexity. While Wilbur is alert to the dark side of human existence, he is more receptive to the brighter emotions of compassion, love and joy. Few American poets since Walt Whitman have offered such compelling optimism.

Wilbur's involvement with the theater began in 1952 when he won a Guggenheim Fellowship to write an original verse drama. Working on his own plays, he despaired. "They didn't come off," he later admitted. "They were very bad, extremely wooden." To learn the craft of verse drama, Wilbur decided to translate an acknowledged masterpiece of the genre, *The Misanthrope* by Jean-Baptiste Poquelin Molière. Little did he guess that he had begun what would eventually grow into a major part of his life's work as well as one of the great translation projects in American literature.

Over the next forty years Wilbur would produce lively, sophisticated and eminently stageworthy versions of Molière's verse comedies: *The Misanthrope* (1955), *Tartuffe* (1963), *The School for Wives* (1971), *The Learned Ladies* (1978), *The School for Husbands* (1992), *The Imaginary Cuckold, or Sganarelle* (1993), *Amphitryon* (1995), *Don Juan* (1998), *The Bungler* (2000) and *Lovers' Quarrels* (2005). The only Molière verse play that has escaped his grasp is *Dom Garcie de Navarre*, which Wilbur concedes is "universally considered a lemon." From the moment his first Molière translation was staged fifty-four years ago, his versions have delighted and impressed audiences. Widely produced from Broadway to college campuses, Wilbur's versions helped create a Molière revival across North America that continues to this day. He also translated two neoclassical verse tragedies by Racine: *Andromache* (1982) and *Phaedra* (1986). More recently he has turned his attention to the works of Corneille.

It would be hard to overpraise Wilbur's special genius for verse translation. Whether re-creating the witty badinage of Molière or the high tragic music of Racine and Corneille, Wilbur has the uncanny ability to create English versions that never feel like translations. They read and play as if they were originally written in English. The same virtue is equally evident in his extensive translations of lyric poetry from French, Italian, Russian and Romanian. (One famous poet told me that Wilbur's translations were as good as her originals—and this was a writer not given to flattery.) The distinction, variety and extent of his efforts have earned him a position as one of the greatest translators in the history of American poetry. His French translations alone fill half a bookshelf.

Happy to leave the drama on the stage, Wilbur has led a generally quiet and settled life. Now eighty-eight, he lives in the same house in Cummington, Massachusetts, that he moved into with his wife and family in 1965. Two years ago, his wife, Charlee, died. They had been married sixty-five years. Wilbur still works almost every day, typing his poems on a venerable L. C. Smith manual. His literary powers remain intimidatingly intact, as two superb new poems in the *New Yorker* this past January amply demonstrate. He has also finished two major theatrical translations from Corneille: A tragedy (*Le Cid*) and a comedy (*The Liar*). These new Corneille versions will be published this summer. Both of them await their first production.

Dana Gioia: How did you first become interested in Molière?

Richard Wilbur: It wasn't in school, where my French studies were all about grammar, a subject to which I've always had a foolish resistance. During World War II, when my division landed in southern France and swept north, I became a halting interpreter for my company, and picked up a book or two to read in transit: something by Pierre Louÿs, some poems of Louis Aragon. After the war, when I went to Harvard on the G.I. Bill, my friends André du Bouchet and Pierre Schneider got me to reading such Frenchmen as Nerval and Villiers de l'Isle-Adam. But it wasn't until 1948, when my wife and I went to Paris on leave from Harvard's Society of Fellows, that I encountered Molière, in a stunning performance of *Le Misanthrope*, starring Pierre Dux, at the Comédie-Française.

What prompted your first translation of Molière?

By 1952, T. S. Eliot and Christopher Fry had brought verse drama to Broadway, and in Cambridge the Poets' Theatre was in high gear. I proposed to the Guggenheim Foundation that I write a verse play, but once I was funded, and established in an adobe study in New Mexico, I proved unripe for the task. It then occurred to me that by translating *The Misanthrope* I could keep my word and learn something.

Can you describe your process of translating Molière?

I read the play, mostly unassisted by scholarship or criticism, and get to know its characters and milieu. Then I render it couplet by couplet, aiming for a maximum fidelity to sense, form and tone. My chief virtue as a translator is stubbornness: I will spend a whole spring day, a perfect day for tennis, getting one or two lines right. Now that I have seen some splendid productions of my Molière translations, I render them in what I hope is the manner of Brian Bedford or Sada Thompson.

What is the hardest part of translating Molière?

The hardest thing is to find, playing with and against the pentameter, just the right timing for a witty or comical line.

Do the rehearsals and production process change your work?

Because my translations are so slavish, I am not asked to do any rewriting at the rehearsal stage. But attending rehearsals and productions has gradually improved my ability to think and feel theatrically.

As a poet, do you think you approach translating Molière differently from the way a playwright might?

I'm sure that a playwright would more quickly visualize the scene, the action, the choreography, the authorized "business." But I would not defer to him about the text. Because Molière's comedies are so thoroughly *written*, I am not likely to be wrong about his drift and tone.

Poetry tends to be a very personal art, while theater is necessarily collaborative. How has the experience in the theater affected your work?

My lyrics for the musical show *Candide* were collaborative, and I enjoyed working with Lenny Bernstein, but I think that my poems were not altered by the process. In doing the Molière translations, however, I know that I have changed as a poet: I am readier to speak out of a single mood or mask, as in "Two Voices in a Meadow" or that long monologue "The Mind-Reader."

How does Molière speak to contemporary American audiences?

Molière's language is readily understood by any American audience. So are the plots of his major comedies, which study the effect of an unbalanced central figure on those about him. Molière's idea of what is normal, natural or balanced is very much like our own, and so there is no need for "updating." I have no patience with the sort of director who, thinking to render Alceste accessible, has him dress and behave like a hippie who "tells it like it is." That did happen once, and I have not forgotten it.

You have also translated plays by Racine and Corneille. Is the old actor's adage true for translation, that playing comedy is harder than tragedy?

I've found it easier to translate Molière's comedies. The spare nobility of Racine is very challenging, and in rendering a heroic play like Corneille's *Le Cid* one has to be careful not to slip into the oratorical.

Have there been particular productions of Molière or your other theatrical works that remain particularly memorable?

There have been fine productions in big towns and small, and throughout our splendid galaxy of repertory theaters. Of course, no later performance could so amaze me as *The Misanthrope*'s premiere at the Poets' Theatre in 1955, in which the poet Peter Davison played the lead. To my great joy, the demand for tickets was such that the show had to be moved from its original garret-like venue to MIT's new auditorium. And then there was the next year's New York production, directed by Stephen Porter at Theatre East, and starring Ellis Rabb and Jackie Brookes.

Has working with any particular actor influenced your approach to translation?

Yes, Brian Bedford has been my friend for many years, and I have seen him in many roles. He was unforgettable as Richard II, to mention but one of his triumphs, and he has been the life of many Molière productions. If I think of him while translating, it enlivens the words and gives me a more palpable sense of the work.

Were there other translations or classical theater that inspired the direction of your own work?

When I was fifteen or so, I saw Walter Hampden do *Cyrano* at some New York playhouse. Whose translation was used I don't know, but I think the experience may have implanted in me the notion that old French plays could be viable in contemporary American theater.

What literary translators do you most admire?

The last century has been a great age of translation, and the list of heroes is too long to recite. Let me say just this: Yesterday

123

I came upon a translation by Miller Williams of a poem by the great Trastevere poet Belli, and said to myself, That's it. It will never have to be translated again.

The translators whom I most esteem are those who do not translate *pro tem*, but work in the wild hope of doing the job once and for all.

You are a singularly remarkable translator of poetry. Why do you devote so much creative energy to translation?

Translation must be faithful, and so it can't be creative *ab ovo*. But at the very least it uses a poet's abilities between the visits of his Muse. I think it can limber his voice and range, and give him great satisfactions and, with luck, can bring him royalties.

Why are there so few literary translations published in the U.S.?

As chairman of the National Endowment for the Arts, you would know better than I whether publishers are reluctant to bring out literary translations. If that is true in all genres, they should be ashamed. As a translator of classic French drama, I have of course often heard the editorial adage, "Plays don't sell."

Do you have any advice for poets or playwrights who want to translate or produce classical theater?

I would urge such translators to do their work faithfully and straight, and to insist on the same qualities in any production. Death to adaptations and adulterations.

Poet Dana Gioia served as chairman of the National Endowment for the Arts from 2004 to 2009. This article was funded by the Sidney E. Frank Foundation. It first appeared in American Theatre *magazine in April 2009.*

Jean-Baptiste Poquelin Molière (1622–1673) was a French playwright and actor. Molière's plays include *The Misanthrope*, *Tartuffe*, *The School for Wives*, *The School for Husbands*, *The Miser*, *Lovers' Quarrels*, *The Imaginary Invalid* and *The Imaginary Cuckold, or Sganarelle*, among others.

Richard Wilbur is author of more than thirty-five books, including works of poetry, translation, prose, children's books and essays. Wilbur is the most prolific and gifted translator of Molière, and is credited with the explosive revival of Molière's plays in North America, beginning in 1955 with *The Misanthrope*. Wilbur's translations of Molière, Racine, Corneille and others are widely praised for incorporating the spirit of both language and author, while maintaining the original form and rhyme scheme. Wilbur is the only living American poet to have won the Pulitzer Prize twice. He has been awarded the National Book Award, the Bollingen Prize, two PEN translation awards and two Guggenheim fellowships. He served as U.S. Poet Laureate. Wilbur taught on the faculties of Harvard, Wellesley, Wesleyan and Smith (where he is poet emeritus). He lives in Cummington, Massachusetts, and is at present the Simpson Lecturer at Amherst College.